College Success Guaranteed

5 Rules to Make It Happen

Malcolm Gauld

ROWMAN & LITTLEFIELD EDUCATION

A division of

ROWMAN & LITTLEFIELD PUBLISHERS, INC.

Lanham • New York • Toronto • Plymouth, UK

Published by Rowman & Littlefield Education
A division of Rowman & Littlefield Publishers, Inc.
A wholly owned subsidiary of
The Rowman & Littlefield Publishing Group, Inc.
4501 Forbes Boulevard, Suite 200, Lanham, Maryland 20706
http://www.rowmaneducation.com

Estover Road, Plymouth PL6 7PY, United Kingdom

British Library Cataloguing in Publication Information Available

Library of Congress Cataloging-in-Publication Data
Gauld, Malcolm, 1954–
  College success guaranteed : 5 rules to make it happen / Malcolm Gauld.
    p. cm.
  ISBN 978-1-61048-042-0 (pbk. : alk. paper) —
  ISBN 978-1-61048-043-7 (electronic)
  1. College student orientation. 2. Study skills. I. Title.
  LB2343.3.G39 2011
  378.1'98—dc22   2011005704

∞™ The paper used in this publication meets the minimum requirements
of American National Standard for Information Sciences—Permanence of
Paper for Printed Library Materials, ANSI/NISO Z39.48-1992.

Printed in the United States of America

To MIKE DAWES
A great teacher and student of life who taught me that
if you want to have a friend, you've got to be a friend.

Contents

"Don't forget to click Reply."

Congratulations!!!

So, you're headed off to college . . . Congratulations! Looks like those twelve-plus years of school are about to pay off . . . Big Time! You should feel proud.

So, tell me, are you ready? I mean, *really* ready?

Before you answer, I feel compelled to warn you that a lot of things have changed since I was in college in the mid-70s. (And in case you're wondering, *No, I was* not *ready*.) Without offering up a list here, I'll just point out what is maybe the most glaring difference: The Cost . . . has increased . . . more than *tenfold*.

To dramatically illustrate, my daughter and I share the same alma mater. What my parents spent (combined with my college loans) to send me there for one year will not cover my daughter's costs . . . for *one month*.

So, back to the readiness question: Are you ready?

No? Then this book offers a simple track to run on. Hope it helps. (I also hope that you don't see my point about the cost as the start of a guilt trip. No more, I promise.)

Yes? Before you dismiss this book as an inappropriate high school graduation gift from someone "who obviously doesn't know me," why not consider it a quick and easy safety check?

But while we're on "yes"—and not to burst your bubble, but . . . how do you know for sure that your "Readiness Detector" is working? In other words, how do you know for sure that you *really* know whether you're ready or not?

I have taught and coached teenagers for over three decades and have watched thousands of them go off to college. Some just take off like rockets from the get-go. Others either fail to launch or crash-and-burn before midterms. Of the latter group, most simply could not summon the discipline to get their act together in order to do what they were supposed to do. However, there were some who were willing to do the work, but simply did not know how to organize themselves now that Mom and/or Dad was not around to hold their feet to the fire. Independent time-management is key.

Although I have given up trying to predict how my students will fare when they head off to college, I have often found myself wishing I could have offered more assistance to those who found out too late that their Readiness Detector had let them down by showing a "false positive" reading. Some of these have sadly found themselves back in their high school living arrangement (i.e., Mom, Dad, and the whole nine yards) with one difference: no school to go to.

Several years ago I began giving a talk to high school seniors a few days before they were to graduate. I called it my "5 Rules for College Survival Talk." That's what this book is about.

In many ways, the book has been inspired by the looks on the faces of the students I have watched return to visit after their first year of college. Some look and seem to exude the feel of vibrant, conquering heroes. Others look and feel . . . well, pretty bummed out. Folks in the first group often say, "You know, those Five Rules helped me out a lot." Folks in the latter group often mumble something about having "fallen off the path." No matter where you fall, I hope this book offers a simple and helpful track to run on, especially in the early going.

That track involves five simple rules that are easy to understand and not all that hard to follow once you commit to them. I'm not claiming that they are all of equal value. As a matter of fact, not only is Rule #1 the hands-down most important of all, it might even be more important than the other four combined. You might even be able to skip one of these rules. (Rule #4 comes to mind, but don't even think about skipping Rule #1!)

I do claim that anyone—*absolutely anyone*—can follow these rules. Think about it. Not everyone can make straight A's, or graduate *magna cum laude*, or make dean's list. But everyone and anyone can follow these rules.

I suspect you will wind up modifying some of the rules in order to suit your learning style or lifestyle preferences. You'll just want to be sure that whatever modifications you ultimately choose to make are based on an objective and accurate understanding of what works (and does not work) best for you. Until you have that understanding, know that I have never encountered anyone who went wrong following these Five Rules as they are presented in this book.

A FEW WORDS ON BULLSHIT

And when it comes to that "understanding," the lifelong teacher in me can't resist going around the bases one more time. I often tell my teenage students that "Man is the only animal in the forest that bullshits himself." Think about it.

Animals pretty much serve their best interests on a daily basis. They generally:

- Sleep when they're tired
- Eat a healthy diet
- Keep trim and stay in good physical condition
- Have no problems with procrastination
- Have a healthy and responsible sex life
- And so forth

Men and women, on the other hand, often have trouble with the above to say nothing of other issues, especially when it comes to:

- Eating and drinking the right things
- Getting enough sleep
- Maintaining exercise routines
- Sticking to schedules
- Over-spending
- And so forth

Animals in the wild *never* have those problems. (They also don't smoke . . . anything.) Not only do men and women have those problems on an all-too-frequent basis, we often delude ourselves into believing that we *don't* have them when we most certainly do. For some of us it can be as simple as trying to feel good about offsetting a high-fat-content fast-food lunch with a diet cola. For others it might be "I never drink before 5" and making up for lost time as soon as the hour strikes. (Chances are you've heard the joke about the guy who says, "Hey, it's 5 o'clock somewhere in the world" as he chugs an early afternoon draft brewski.)

By the time we hit college, most of us have developed sensors to help us detect bullshit when it is being served up to us by others. However, we sometimes fall short when it comes to detecting our propensity to serve it up to . . . ourselves. For many, college is the first place where this life skill becomes critical for surviving, much less thriving.

Getting back to some of those kids who end up bummed out and living at home with "Mom, Dad, and the whole nine yards," I have often seen that many of those young men and women are the last to know when the ship is indeed going down. Sadly, right up until the eleventh hour, some will say to themselves, their friends, or their parents:

- "Plenty of kids miss a lot more classes than I do."
- "I don't party anywhere near as much as the hockey players do."
- "I'm really going to buckle down . . . *next* week."
- "Professor X never flunks anyone."
- "I already went over most of the class material in high school."

And so it goes until they find out too late that they have been bullshitting themselves the whole time, and they are the last to know. The problem with bullshitting yourself is simply the fact that it's hard to know when you're doing it. (It's weird, but bullshit has an uncanny way of protecting itself.) So, why not play it safe? Cover your bets and assume at the start that you have a fairly high capacity for bullshitting yourself. How? Follow these Five Rules until you know for sure.

Much of the wisdom in the following pages comes from current and recently graduated college students from over thirty different colleges and universities who were nice enough to share their successes and failures with me for your benefit. I simply sat down and talked with them, asked them some standard questions, and then listened and took a lot of notes. I'm not guaranteeing that every piece of advice in this book will work for you. As a matter of fact, it's only fair for me to warn you that in offering up their stories, some of my interviewees even served up ideas and suggestions that were contradictory. (This was especially true when it came to study routines.) My guarantee is far more basic: If you earnestly strive to honor the Five Rules in this book, you'll not only have no trouble maintaining "student in good-standing" status at the college of your choice, you'll feel good about your college experience. (Your parents will too, and that can really come in handy when you come home for breaks.)

The college experience is a very special one. For generations, many people have described it as "the best four years of my life." I don't know if that will be true for you, but look at it this way: There's got to be a reason why so many people have said that.

During one interview, a recent Kenyon College graduate said, "Those four years of college are the most selfish years of your life. It's the first stab at real life, the first time that you find yourself in a community that is external to home, your family, and your hometown community. You never forget it!" With that in mind, you might do well to have a plan of attack. That's what this simple book is about.

Oh, and not to burst your bubble again, but you should expect all of your books in college to be a lot thicker and more complex than this one. My hope is that some attention paid to this short and simple book might help you tackle all those other long, thick intimidating ones.

Introduction

What this book is
What this book is not

This is a "do" book. It is not a "don't" book . . . Huh?

This book focuses on five simple things you need to "do" after you enroll in college.

It pretty much omits the "don'ts," the negative actions you should avoid. I take this approach for two reasons.

First, by now you have already gotten an earful of "don'ts" from a whole list of people who care about you: parents, grandparents, siblings, friends, uncles, aunts, cousins, teachers, coaches, counselors, therapists, etc. I don't need to steal their fire.*

Second, I remember how much I listened to that stuff when I was headed off to college . . . not much.

My claim is short and sweet: If you follow these five rules, you will not get one of those pink slips during the semester break informing you not to return for the following semester. While it's possible that these simple guidelines will be enough for you to make dean's list, I'm not making that promise. You may need to do more than what is outlined here in order to make dean's list. You may even get away with less. I'm simply saying that over the past few decades, I've seen a fair number of sad nineteen-year-olds who have just flunked out, and I've yet to see one in that group who had followed these rules. So, what are the rules? Glad you asked. You just might be ready for Rule #1.

But not so fast . . .

Just so those folks don't think I'm shirking my responsibilities or ducking out of the dirty work, I offer this thought: If your child or loved one honors the Five Rules, they won't have the time or inclination to do all that much that they shouldn't do. That's between me and you. Hey, we both know that kids skip the footnotes.

Pop Quiz
What's 168?

Before we launch into Rule #1, I ask you to consider a number: 168.

I've got two questions for you:

Question #1: *What's the significance of this number?*

- Number of school days in a year? No.
- Average number of campus-wide keg parties in a school year? No. (Ah, maybe we need to revisit the "don't" idea?)
- Number of books you'll need to buy in your first year. Nope. (But it may feel like it.)

Answer #1: *The number of **hours in a week** ($24 \times 7 = 168$).*

Question #2: *In order to ensure your stable and productive enrollment in college, what is a reasonable number of hours for you to sacrifice?*

- 84? (You're thinking half, right?) No. (But you're going to like this book.)
- 50? No. (But I like your attitude.)
- 42? (You're thinking 25%?) No. (But I like your math.)
- 10? No. (Again, about that "don't" idea . . .)

Answer #2: *27*

Commit 27 non-negotiable hours to this plan. The downside? You get no say when it comes to these hours. The upside? You get 141 hours left over to use as you wish. Rule #3 will call on you to give up a few of these, but you will decide solely on your own how they will be spent. On to Rule #1.

College Success
Guaranteed

"Don't cry, Mom. Lots of parents have children who didn't get into their first-choice college, and they went on to live happy, fulfilled lives."

1

Rule #1: Go to Class

> "80% of life is showing up."
>
> —Woody Allen

The first rule has three words: 1 = GO. 2 = TO. 3 = CLASS. GO to class. Go TO class. Go to CLASS.

Emphasize whichever word you want. Just GO!

You're thinking: "Duh! Tell me something I don't know." Read on. We're going to spend some time on this one.

While all five rules are important, this one might well be more important than the other four . . . combined.

I'll even go out on a limb and say that if you were to choose to pay close attention to this one and mere lip service to the others, you *might* still do OK. However, if you were to choose to faithfully honor, say #2 and #3, while ignoring #1, you very well might flunk out.

Let's explore this rule more deeply. Before you begin to think about yourself as a student, give some thought to the people who will be teaching you—your professors. What makes them tick, anyway? You'll notice some differences between them and your high school teachers.

WHAT'S UP WITH THESE PROFESSORS, ANYWAY?

Professorial Priorities

Here's one difference between your high school teachers and your professors: Your high school teachers care about you first and the subjects they teach second.

Most people choose to teach high school because they really like kids. Even those who are passionate about the subjects they teach tend to set their priorities with kids first, subject second.

To be on the safe side, assume that your college professors will value these priorities in reverse. That is, they will care about their subject first and you second.

This is not to say that your professors will lack dedication to your progress and happiness, and it's not a criticism of professors so much as a reminder that you are now an adult and your college instructors will expect you to function as such. They are pursuing their subjects with a deep passion, and they will expect you to do the same. Hopefully, some of your professors will become lifelong mentors, maybe even future ushers or bridesmaids in your wedding. (Relax, I won't mention marriage again.) However, you may well encounter some who even regard you as an inconvenience. (To tell you the truth, I hope you do because the experience will provide a meaningful and instructive educational opportunity that will take on increasing value once you leave college for the world of work.)

Through Their Eyes

If you're reading this book, you're probably trying to start thinking like a college student. Stop for a moment, and try thinking like a professor instead. Think about this whole college thing through their eyes.

Let's assume for a moment that your deepest passion in life is nineteenth-century French poetry. You eat, sleep, and drink it. As a college student, you studied in Paris. As a graduate student, you spent hours in various French libraries poring over obscure poems. Let's say you then pursued this interest all the way to a Ph.D.

Eventually you need to get a job. What are your options? Well, you could write a bestseller (à la Harry Potter with a French twist) that will set you up for life. (Not likely.) OK, maybe you could write a screenplay for a blockbuster film about . . . *drum roll* . . . nineteenth-century French poets. (Ah . . . don't think so.)

After weighing your options, chances are you'll enter into discussions with a college or university in hopes of landing a deal that goes something like this: You *get* access to a great library, subscriptions to French poetry journals, maybe an administrative assistant, computer access, scholarly colleagues, a salary with health and pension benefits, the opportunity to attend conferences, stuff like that. In exchange for these things, you *give* (i.e., teach) two courses per semester on nineteenth-century French poetry.

Now, let's assume that you the reader, a rookie college student, enroll in one of these nineteenth-century French poetry courses. It's entirely possible that your professor will be highly dedicated to you and your fellow students. Let's hope so. However, it's also possible that this professor will be so engrossed in French poetry that he or she will be oblivious to you, to say nothing of being unconcerned with the unique "learning style" that your parents and high school teachers so carefully nurtured, some to the point of obsession. Hey, maybe your professor won't even like you. So, cover your bets. Be prepared for this very scenario. How? Follow Rule #1 . . . GO TO CLASS!

Profs = Refs

In addition to teaching for many years, I also coached soccer, basketball, and lacrosse. When I started coaching, I focused solely on my players—how they were performing, individually and collectively. Before long, I began to realize that I also had to pay attention to the referees as it became clear that they sometimes played a much bigger role in the outcome of some of the games than I had considered. I quickly concluded that staying on their good side was wise.

Eventually it began to dawn on me that referees do not call fouls. Instead, they blow their whistles when they see an action that *looks like* a foul. There's a big difference.

When the basketball goes out of bounds in a hotly contested game, there is no way that the referee can always know for sure whether or not it deflected, ever so slightly, off your opponent's fingertips a split second after your errant pass intended for a breaking teammate. To add to his consternation, he's got you and your opponent passionately pointing in opposite directions of the court, each of you pleading your case as the rightful recipient of the ball. With the roar of a partisan crowd blasting in his ears, the referee must make his best call, an educated and decisive guess, but he very well might not know for sure.

After I had coached for a while, I came to believe that my team would receive more favorable calls if the referees liked me—or, at least, if they did not *dis*like me too much. So I took pains to be pleasant toward them. Although I can't say for sure that this approach got my teams more favorable calls, there was no downside to it. It definitely improved civility and set a better example for sportsmanship.

I remember one of our star players who would sometimes incorporate a brief chat with the referee into his pre-game warm-up ritual. After doing layups, jump shots, and foul shots with the team, he would sidle over and inquire about the well-being of the ref and his family. While he believed that it helped his game, I know that he came across as a gentleman and made both our team and school look good. What's not to like?

By now you can probably figure out where I'm going with this. Treat your professors the way this young man treated the referees in his games. Be present. Be pleasant. Make eye contact. Appear enthusiastic and interested. What have you got to lose?

During my teaching years when I would assess final grades and comments, I sometimes found myself thinking, "Boy, this kid works so hard! I'd love to try to find him/her a few more points." I also confess that there were times when I thought, "It kills me to give this kid a good grade because he/she has such a poor attitude." Now, I like to think that my better self ruled in both circumstances, but . . . who knows?

Professors, like refs, are human beings. If you are nice to them, they will probably be nice to you. This could well have an impact on your grade.

GO TO CLASS
(DEFINITELY DO NOT PASS GO)
GO DIRECTLY TO CLASS

Early on during the scores of conversations I had with college students and young alums, I quickly noticed that contradictory observations were common. One student's helpful ritual was another's straitjacket of suffering. At the same time, I would note that I did not encounter a single student or alum who didn't agree that attending all your classes is a very, very good idea. In fact, those who experimented with absenteeism uniformly regretted it on some level. In short, either their grades suffered or they simply didn't learn as much as they might have. Rather than judge the various approaches different students utilize to help themselves get to class and get something out of being there, I offer them here without comment. (Well, that is, aside from an occasional irresistible barb here and there.) The key is to align yourself with an approach that will work for you.

OK, here we go.

It's What You (or Your Parents!) Are Paying For

In recent years, I have invited the parents of the graduates to sit in on my annual talk to their children. One year a parent told me that she had taken the time to figure out exactly how much each of her child's classes would cost her. Try this yourself. Add up the number of classes you will take during the semester and then divide that number into the amount you are paying in tuition. Even if you exclude the cost of room and board, the per-class cost is a scary figure. Even scarier if you're sleeping through the class.

A Colby College grad said,

> Colby was expensive. The way I saw it, I'm here to get an education and when you get right down to it, the classes are the primary vehicle I need to use in order to get it. The books we read I could have bought and read elsewhere. There are also plenty of libraries around my hometown. If I wanted nice work-out facilities, I could have joined an awesome gym somewhere near home for a lot less money. I certainly could find other places besides an expensive college whenever I felt the need to socialize and party. However, the actual classes were the one-of-a-kind benefit I was receiving for the tuition dollars my parents and I were spending. After all, the only place I could take *those* courses was at *this* college. Therefore, in order to get my money's worth, I needed to attend all of my classes.

A student from Notre Dame concurred, "I have a certain amount of disbelief over the fact that my parents are spending $50,000 a year for me to go to class. So, the least I can do is, well, go to class. I have assured my parents that no matter what, I will hold up my end of that obligation. And good things tend to flow from that decision." As far as words to the wise go, I can't improve upon those.

Schedule for Success

A New York University (NYU) student advised, "Don't make an unrealistic schedule." He reasoned,

> I'm a late sleeper. I accept that about myself. And so as much as possible, I try to have a class schedule that permits me to do just that: sleep late. When I first got to college, I had a lot of early classes, and I tended to miss a lot of them. With a schedule of mostly late morning classes, I find that I make most of them. Therefore, at the beginning of each semester when I sign up for courses, I plan accordingly.

A student from Southern Methodist University (SMU) concurred with the NYU student, noting that his preference was "not too early, not too late" when it comes to class. He, too, sees himself as a mid-morning person. So, he tries to synchronize his daily classes in alignment with his own personal sweet spot.

A student at the University of North Carolina (UNC), Greensboro, told me, "I select a class schedule that's convenient for *me*. I'm paying for it, so I get to pick when I go." He seemed to steal a page from the NYU student when he noted that he tries to schedule classes between 11:00 and 3:30. "I especially like back-to-back classes, one right after the other."

Control What You Can Control

Here's one from the "Know Thyself" category. A student at Furman University told me,

Before I even arrived at college, I had already fully accepted the fact that I am a bad test-taker. I quickly saw that I needed to focus on what I can control and not worry so much about those things I can't. I might not be able to control how well I perform on midterms and finals—*Hey, even if I think my essay is great, there's no guarantee that the professor will agree*—but I definitely can control whether or not I go to class. So, I go.

This Furman student went on to say, "If you select classes according to the subjects that you're passionate about, you're more likely to go to class. If nothing else, you'll at least want to see what happens next."

A recent grad from William & Mary put it even more succinctly: "No matter what the class was, at the beginning, I knew two things to be true: (1) I didn't know the material; and (2) I don't like reading. So I went to class."

Perhaps looking through the other end of the telescope, a Washington & Lee grad offered a blunt acknowledgment: "I was not diligent with class attendance. If I liked the topic, I went. If not, I didn't. And I'd have to say that my grades indeed reflected my attendance." Plain and simple.

Attendance and Grades

One parent, a sociology professor, approached me after a recent talk and told me that he had done a comparative analysis of his students' grades in comparison with their attendance records. His conclusion: On average, his students lost two points on their final grade for every class they missed. That's a scary figure. It's also easily remedied: Go to Class!

Sequence and Memory Triggers

A Vassar graduate pointed out that many courses are sequential in nature. If you miss a class, you fall out of sequence, and the next one you attend might very well build upon knowledge that was transmitted in the class that you missed.

Emphasizing a consideration similar to the sequence factor, a recent graduate from St. Lawrence University told me that she found class attendance was of critical importance due to what she called "memory triggers." Professors during class often make their points with inside jokes, references, and nuances that can trigger your memory to more complicated points and concepts. Fail to attend class, and you will not internalize these nuances and memory triggers.

The memory trigger can also visit the teacher and, in turn, boomerang back as a benefit to the student. For example, a University of Maine alum told me that he always sat in the same seat, and when he went to the professor for office hours, the professor tended to remember him. As a result, he is convinced that the professor's memory trigger of his attendance and interest was a positive one which helped his grade.

The same University of Maine graduate told me that, although he regrets the fact that he didn't always study as hard as he could have, he made it a practice to attend all of his classes. In one class a Nobel Laureate showed up and spoke to the class. Not only did this student get to see and hear a fascinating presentation, he later discovered that much of what the laureate had said during his presentation wound up on the final exam. Had he missed the class, not only would he have missed out on these benefits, he would have been left trying to get someone who did attend the class to relay to him what happened—and that's only if he knew ahead of time that it was going to be on the exam—and secondhand is never as good as firsthand. Allow me to say that again: *Secondhand is never as good as firsthand.*

Leave the Laptop in the Dorm . . . Cell Phone Too

A majority of the students I spoke with noted that laptops and other technological devices are a double-edged sword. On the one hand, you can't live without them in terms of research, communications with professors, getting cyber-updates, and typing papers. On the other hand, more than a few students admitted that during a boring lecture in a cavernous auditorium it can be awfully tempting to Facebook a friend back home or play a video game. ("Maybe just this once won't hurt . . .")

Being of the analog generation, I had naturally assumed that the students I spoke with would refer to both the Internet and the many clever toys that access it with unbridled joy and reverence. In fact, this assumption was only strengthened on a recent stroll through the campus of George Washington University when seemingly every student I passed was jabbering with passion and purpose—cell phone pinned to one ear with one hand while the other hand cradled books or portfolios—all the while simultaneously negotiating their way through urban auto and pedestrian traffic on their way to class. Not so. In fact, I'd estimate that negative comments outweighed positive ones by a factor of more than two to one. Here are a range of comments on things cyber.

An NYU student simply said, "When you go to class, leave the laptop at home." He noted that while he might have initially envisioned a paperless college experience, he ultimately learned to take temptation off the table and limit himself to *only* a pen and paper when he went to class. He said, "While a pen and paper may seem primitive in today's world, there's no way they'll navigate you over to Facebook."

A student from SMU echoed the laptop observation, "Every time I bring the laptop to class, I end up on Facebook. So, I just don't bring it."

A Colby grad told me that he always took hand-written notes. He said, "There was something about having a computer screen between me and the teacher that created a disconnect in my learning. I just found that I remembered stuff I wrote down in a notebook a lot better than the information I saw on a computer screen."

A student from Tufts University told me that he had stopped using his laptop for note-taking and switched to a three-ring binder. He is convinced that the very act of writing, just by itself, causes him to pay closer attention and gives him a better chance of remembering a given fact or concept later if it comes up on a test.

A Hobart College student agreed, "The simple muscular movement of writing with pen on paper contributes to enhanced memory." A student from Notre Dame said simply, "I take a notebook and pen and nothing else to class."

A recent Boston College grad went a step further, noting that some Boston College professors flat out prohibited laptops. "We all pretty much just left them in our dorms," she said.

The Notre Dame student also stressed the importance of turning off the phone. While it's an obvious and absolute no-no to have your phone ring during class, this student said, "Professors absolutely hate it when they see you texting during class." And, of course, even if a professor doesn't see you, you are definitely not going to remember what the professor is talking about if you're texting your buddy back home.

Dress for Success

A student at the University of California (UC), Berkeley, told me that it was important to dress properly. When I regarded him quizzically, he noted that he had a simple rule: No Sweats and No Flip-Flops. He discovered that a polo shirt gave him some semblance of professionalism, and he found that this ensemble allowed him to pay closer attention to what was going on in class. (This reminded me of a friend during my own college days who would actually put on a tie when he was having trouble concentrating. Although his friends razzed him mercilessly, he swore that it worked for him.) The UC Berkeley student also noted that he had a better attendance record and a stronger attention span when he had showered, eaten breakfast, and had a cup of coffee. That is his ritual, and he is convinced that his attendance and attention span benefit when he follows it.

A recent graduate of Boston College told me a story about dressing for class that demonstrates the flip side of the UC Berkeley student's reasoning. Being a Division 1 athlete, she routinely found herself in sweats for several hours a day. Initially, she was afraid that wearing them to class would cause her professors to brand her with the dreaded label of the "dumb jock." To counter the stereotype, she intentionally always sat in the front row and made it a point to speak up often in class discussions. She found that this earned her respect from her professors, many of whom came to her basketball games, supporting her off and on the court. In effect, rather than attempt to disguise her uniqueness, she placed it front-and-center, and it worked out well for her.

On a more humorous note, an SMU student quipped that he liked to wear the same hat to class every day. While he would take it off once class started, he was convinced that the teacher recognized him by his hat. "It can't hurt," he reasoned.

MORE REASONS TO GO TO CLASS . . .
(SOME OF THEM QUIRKY)

Cantaloupe Day and Other Professorial Perks

I spoke with several college students who noted that their professors had developed some unique perks to incentivize class attendance, essentially prizes for the simple act of show-ing up. Here are four examples.

Cantaloupe Day

A student at Lawrence University told of a professor who, when sensing low class attendance, might offer a secret word that he would make known only to those actually in atten-dance at that moment. The students were told to remember the word and informed that they would be asked to divulge it and would receive extra credit during an upcoming exam. In one case the word was "cantaloupe." Days or weeks later at the test, only those students who wrote "cantaloupe" in the extra-credit space received the bonus. Those who missed class on "Cantaloupe Day" lost out.

A first-year student at Bates College related the same story, different word. During one particular class session, atten-dance was sparse due to an apparently campus-wide celebra-tion the night before. The professor disclosed to those present that there would be a surprise quiz later that week. He then advised them that they would be wise to remember the word "Kelly." (Although I never found out, I presume that this might have been the name of his spouse, mother, daughter, or dog.) A few days later, the professor handed out the quiz to the class. The final question asked the students to write down the secret word that had been divulged earlier in the week. He also announced that those who knew the answer would get 100% on the quiz. This particular student was glad that he had been present that day. What else can I say, Go to Class!

100% Bonus for Attendance

A University of Maryland student told me that she had a professor who became angry when class attendance would dip to low numbers on very nice spring days. On such days, the professor might pass out a sheet of paper numbered from one to five with five corresponding blank lines. The students were instructed to sign their name and pass it up to the front. All students in attendance received a 100% that was figured into their final grade.

Grading Up for Showing Up

A University of Denver student noted that some professors were known to gather all the grades of students who were on the cusp between an A and a B and would then add class attendance into the mix. Those with perfect or near-perfect attendance would fall to the A side, and those without it would fall to B.

Similarly, a UNC Greensboro poetry professor announced at the beginning of the course that perfect attendance would be rewarded with the student's grade being raised one point. In other words, a B would become a B+, a C- would become a C, and so on. And all you had to do was show up.

Cleveland Browns Bonus

A Hobart College student noted that there are all sorts of things going on in a class that you can only take in if you are present. (Again, those Memory Triggers.) For example, he noted that one professor sometimes threw in personal information about his favorite football team or his place of birth and would actually ask questions related to these random factoids for extra credit. He did this simply to check to see if you were attending class. The Hobart student said, "So, if you were in attendance, you would likely recall that he was a Cleveland Browns fan and that he hailed from Shaker Heights. If you didn't know that, then the professor safely assumed that you had not been showing up for class."

STILL MORE REASONS

Attend Class, Learn Something

While the above examples may be clear-cut incentives highlighting a direct benefit to diligent class attendance, students invariably come to find that the benefit of attending class actually has a broader value which is realized over time. First off (and simply put), you will learn more if you attend class than if you don't. (What a concept!)

Cost of Missing Class

A student at Hobart College told me that he initially adopted a policy where he always went to class at the beginning of the semester. He would get the class understanding down to a manageable rhythm and then he would rest on his laurels and allow himself to miss some classes. However, he also found out that no matter how on top of things you think you are, as he put it, "If you're not there, you don't know." (Again, *do not bullshit thyself!*)

Small Is Beautiful

A Furman University student told me that the very choice of a relatively small school incentivized her to go to class. She said, "Not only is it obvious when I'm absent, but the professor might well call me and ask me what was wrong."

A Colby grad concurred: "Colby is a small school and professors would call you in to their offices and ask why you were absent! Better to avoid the hassle and just go."

SOME WAYS TO GET THERE

Eat Breakfast

A student at Springfield College told me, "If I miss breakfast, I'm likely to miss class." Therefore, she reasoned that the best way to get to class was to make sure that she made it to breakfast. Too often when she would try to steal thirty more minutes of sleep by missing breakfast, she would either sleep right through class or doze off after she got there.

A Colby grad agreed: "Even if it was only a bagel, without something in my morning stomach, I'd get grumpy in class."

The Case for Mandatory Attendance

A recent graduate from Franklin & Marshall College told me about a fairly fool-proof approach to ensure class attendance:

In her early college years, she intentionally limited her choices to classes where attendance was mandatory. She simply took temptation off the table.

Hockey Fights Off Hookie

A graduate of Worcester State College had a simple way to ensure class attendance. He played ice hockey and had to get up at 6:00 AM for the only available team ice time. After practice, he showered and went to class. Why not get up and get going? (Looking ahead, you will see that this strategy fits with Rule #3: [*Don't Just Sit There*] *Commit to Something.*)

This same student also told me that at one point his grade was stuck between an A and a B. His professor pulled him into his office and said simply, "You have worked so hard in this class that I am going to have your grade fall onto the side of A." While such an approach might not always result in an A, it's a safe bet to assume that failing to attend class is an approach that will not.

Busted by the Coach

Citing another value of playing team sports, a woman who had played Division 1 basketball at Boston College told me that her coach often did spot checks on class attendance by randomly showing up at the actual classes herself. She added, "If you weren't there, you paid for it later that day at practice!"

The Night Before

Our UNC Greensboro student noted that before he turns in for the night, he places his books and notebooks for the following day in his backpack and then places his shoes right next to the bag. He says, "I wake up, get dressed, head for the door, and I'm good to go."

Assume That You'll Be Missed

A recent Yale graduate told me simply, "Assume that the professors are going to take their classes seriously. After all, it's what they have chosen to do with their lives. So, it only stands to reason that if you're not there, everyone knows that."

AFTER YOU GET THERE

First Quartile Rule

During the first class, add up the number of seating rows in the classroom or lecture hall, divide by four, and sit in the first quartile. In other words, if there are twenty-eight rows, sit somewhere in the first seven. I recommend that you sit in the same seat each class, maintain eye contact with the professor, pay attention, take notes, ask questions, make comments, and so forth. Let the professor know that that is your seat, and that you are always present. This will make a favorable impression. You'll also learn more. (Again . . . what a concept!) Let's explore that favorable impression idea a bit more.

Engagement

Steadfast attendance at class will help you in many ways. It is also the best way to forge relationships with professors. I remember a student in the early 2000s who distinguished himself at our school as an athlete, student, and leader. When he headed off to Gettysburg College, he had perhaps defined himself as a lacrosse player. Then, shortly after his arrival, he experienced what he called "the worst week of my life." First, he learned that he had received a failing grade on a biology test. While still reeling from that setback, he was summoned to the lacrosse coach's office to learn that he had been cut from the team. He felt both shattered and uncertain as to how to proceed.

Rather than take pains to avoid his biology professor, the approach he was tempted to take, he instead made a beeline for his office, established a bond with him, and designed a program of study for the remainder of the semester. As the semester progressed, he met regularly with his professor, studied prodigiously, and completed the semester with a strong grade.

As an antidote to his disappointment relative to lacrosse, he poured his energy into other activities, especially his fraternity where he served as Rush Chairman. In short, these setbacks, though jarring at first, evolved into opportunities once he had accepted them as such. Facing a closed door, his initiative caused another to open.

Raise Your Hand

A Vassar graduate told me that she honored a simple rule: Raise your hand at least once per class. She believes that this simple rule provided three benefits:

1. It made time go so much faster, especially in lecture-type classes where the professor's voice can become monotonous.

2. She invariably found that her comments sparked discussion which made the class come alive with intellectual energy.
3. She is convinced that this approach improved her grade because the professor perceived her as someone engaged in the class.

A student at the University of New Hampshire told me that he committed himself to being a regular participant in class discussions because it helped him "stay in the game" and not nod off. This also enabled him to become well-known to his professors. As a junior he found that a number of the advanced classes that he wanted to take were normally limited to seniors. He was able to gain admittance to all of these classes, and he believes it was due to the relationships he had forged with his professors due to his regular participation. So, therefore, class participation is of multi-faceted value as you head off to college.

When I inquired about tricks of the trade for getting more out of class, a Hampshire College student said, "I talk a lot in class. In fact, I think I have a much better time than my classmates do. I also keep eye contact throughout. All the professors know me and all in all, I think that's a good thing on several fronts."

Name Game

A Tufts student also mentioned that he always tried to make a point for the teacher to know his name, reasoning that, if the teacher knew his name, it was easier to demonstrate that he was working hard.

On a similar note, an SMU student stressed: Make sure you go to office hours at least once with each of your professors per semester. He reasoned, "Even if you only go once, it will leave a memorable impression because most students don't go at all."

WHAT TO DO WHEN YOU BREAK RULE #1

No matter how seriously you honor Rule #1, the time will come when you will, in fact, miss a class. When this happens, many new college students are often surprised by what does *not* happen: No axe falls on their heads. Some think, "Hey, that wasn't so bad." They do it again. No repercussions. The spiral begins.

For some, it becomes easier and easier to miss future classes. Before they know it, they find themselves raising their head off the pillow, opening one eye, and pleading with a roommate who is headed out the door, "Hey, Dude, take good notes. You know I'd do the same for you." And, as the song goes, "another one bites the dust."

A UNC Greensboro student noted that whenever he does need to miss a class, he e-mails the professor telling him/her so and why. On one such occasion, he told his professor that he would be attending a music festival rather than attending his class. Rather than chastise him or act insulted, the next time the professor saw him, he simply asked how the festival was. Overall, the professor was impressed that the student thought enough of both him and the class to contact him ahead of time with an honest reason.

So, if you get in a slump, fix it: Go to Class. Sit up front. Make eye contact with the professor. Let the professor see that you are present and engaged.

A Vassar graduate seemed to steal a page from our Gettysburg graduate in noting that when she had to miss class she always made it a point to approach the professor and ask about topics of discussion that were covered in class. This way she was able to pick up on the knowledge that was transmitted but also maintain that all-important relationship.

THE ONLY ACCEPTABLE EXCUSE I EVER HEARD

While you can probably tell that I pretty much regard all excuses for missing class with suspicion, if not outright doubt, I admit that I can see some wisdom to the one excuse that an SMU student allows himself: "There is one condition under which I will allow myself to miss a class, and that is when an important test is taking place that same day in another class." On such occasions, he allows himself to miss a class in order to study for the test, believing that this method helps him stay focused by preventing unrelated information from another class from clouding his thinking. In any case, he tries to limit himself to this one exception in terms of class attendance.

Bonus Tip: Beware of Book-Buying

A Tufts student suggests that you attend four or five classes before you buy any of the books. You will quickly see that you can spend a tremendous amount of money on books, and in some cases you will only be reading a chapter. By waiting to see what you actually need to buy, you can save money and perhaps trade off with classmates and share access to books that will be used to a lesser degree.

SIMPLEST TERMS

During one of my final interview sessions, I found myself sitting in a campus coffee shop with a trio of Bowdoin College students. Before asking any questions, I gave a quick overview of the Five Rules. I was struck by how they simply took it for granted that class attendance was a must. End of discussion. While we went on to debate the merits and finer points of the other four rules, it was striking to me how there was just no discussion about the first one. Word to the wise!

Reducing Rule #1 to its simplest terms: If you had to choose between attending all of your classes and doing none of your homework OR doing all of your homework and attending none of your classes, choose the first option. (However, I urge you to pose dilemmas of a higher order!) But while we're on homework (and BTW, that's a high school term that you won't hear again), this is a good time to move on to Rule #2.

At the end of the day, whether your motivation is to improve your grade or for higher intellectual purposes, attending class is filled with upside and has no downside. So, I repeat, whatever you do when you go to college, Go to Class!

DO THE MATH

Before we move to Rule #2, let's look at the math: 168 − 12 = 156. Most classes meet three hours per week (typically, 60 minutes on MWF or 90 minutes on TU/TH). So, if you take four classes, that adds up to 12 hours per week, leaving you with 156 hours. I'm about to take 15 more.

2

Rule #2: 3 by 5

> "I will *study* and get ready, and maybe my chance will come."
>
> —Abraham Lincoln

STUDY THREE HOURS PER DAY, FIVE DAYS PER WEEK

Even if you happen to have very permissive parents, high school life is highly structured compared to college. For example, if you skip a lot of high school classes or miss homework assignments, *someone* will take notice and call your parents, give you detention, or both.

When you move to college, you are transitioning to an environment where you can easily drown in free time. And sometimes you'll be the last to know. Skip class and you may be the only one who knows about it. You may not have any assignments (and, oh yeah, that's also a high school term) due for a month or more. Before you think "That's awesome!" think again.

The danger is that you could succumb to the temptation of falling into a habit of postponing daily obligations due to a false belief that you have unlimited time to make them up later. At your age, a semester feels like a decade. (Wait until you're my age, and it feels like a week!)

Rule #2 demands a seemingly simple commitment: study three hours per day, five days per week. You are allotted two days when you don't have to do anything.

I recommend that your study hours occur after the last class of the day (i.e., cramming for a quiz in between classes doesn't count). As for those who tell you not to go out on weeknights, I'm not even going there. (Remember, this is a "do" talk.) If you feel a need to go out and work on your DJ skills every night of the week, you will still be able to do that. If that's what you want to do, then study from 4:00 to 5:30, catch some dinner, return to the library at 7:00 and study until 8:30, and you have the rest of the night free.

A Caveat: No Stockpiling

Don't stockpile hours. In other words, if inspiration causes you to study four hours on Monday, do not reward yourself by only studying two hours on Tuesday. Do the full three hours on Tuesday, the whole time congratulating yourself for being such a scholar!

HOMEWORK VS. SYLLABUS

Another critical difference between high school and college is that high school teachers tend to give daily assignments whereas college professors typically hand out a syllabus during the first class of the semester. The syllabus might inform you that nothing is due for weeks at a time.

Imagine that on September 1, the professor stands before you and your classmates and says something like this: "The syllabus indicates the books we're going to read during the semester. . . . We'll have a midterm exam on October 20. . . . You have a ten-page paper due on December 1. . . . Our final exam (which will account for 30 percent of your grade) is scheduled for December 15. . . . So, good luck, and we'll see you on October 20. . . . In the meantime, my office hours are posted on my office door. [More on this later.] Drop by then if you need some extra help. . . . Class dismissed."

Time Commitment vs. Assignment Completion

Rule #2 demands that you commit to a broad time period as opposed to the more narrow objective of assignment completion. So, start assembling the research books you will use on a paper that is due two months from now. . . . Read, read, read! Review notes and readings for an upcoming test. . . . Again, fifteen hours per week may not be sufficient for some to excel at college, and it will be more than enough for others. Just don't let yourself slip below that fifteen-hour time commitment per week.

POINTS OF DISAGREEMENT

In the course of writing this book I interviewed scores of college students and recent grads from close to forty different colleges and universities. After a while it dawned on me that I was dealing with two different audiences: I was talking with veteran students who had "figured it out" in hopes of acquiring some wisdom that I could then pass along to a different audience—one that was experiencing college for the very first time.

Many of the students and recent grads I interviewed arrived at their understanding after trying a number of unsuccessful strategies and approaches. (A few even told stories of learning the hard way after meeting with academic or disciplinary disaster.) While I didn't encounter any students who didn't concur with the essential importance of going to all your classes (or put it this way, I didn't hear any excuses that were not ridiculous!), I found that opinions vary greatly in regard to the best ways to study. Here are four points of contention that repeatedly presented themselves during my interviews.

Group vs. Individual Study

Whereas some students spoke passionately about the benefits of group study, others insisted that the only way to really get anything done, to say nothing of committing important information to memory for test-taking purposes, was to get off by one's self in isolated concentration. For what it's worth, I conclude that you will be wise to develop effective techniques in utilizing both approaches as the need for one or the other will sometimes be dictated by the professor's expectations. Just make sure that you're doing the right one at the right time!

Library: To Go or Not to Go?

On another point, some students said, "I *always* go to the library if I really need to get something done," and others said, "I *never* go to the library because it's too much of a social center." There was even a compromise position: "If I go to the library, I either go to the basement or to the top floor. I definitely stay away from the main floor because it's little more than a major hang-out center, and I can never get anything done there."

Music: Yay or Nay?

Music is another dividing line. Some students are convinced that listening to music enhances their concentration. Others say it's nothing more than a distraction. There was even a common compromise position on this point: "I listen only to *instrumental* music (i.e., classical or jazz) with no lyrics." Students in this boat seem to find that a vocalist causes their concentration to move from the words in the assigned book to the ones in the song, whereas tunes without the words don't disrupt the study process. You'll have to judge for yourself.

Technology: Pros and Cons

The technology issue came up with several of the students I interviewed. A New York University (NYU) student told me that technology can be an accident waiting to happen. On the one hand, sometimes you have to use it. On the other hand, it is very easy to find that your browser has drifted over to Facebook and realize that for the past hour and fifteen minutes all you have done is communicate with your friends back home.

A Set Time and Place

In talking with college students about their study habits, it seems that there are as many techniques as there are students. Pretty much all of the students I spoke with stressed the importance of having a set time in a set location for studying and typically found that their academic work suffered when they strayed from this structure.

Know Thyself

As you no doubt have figured out, a recurring theme in this book is . . . you must know thyself. Then the trick is to transform this personal understanding into a design that fits with what you know to be true about yourself. While you're working on figuring that system out, I urge you to follow a very simple rule, one that will require you to sacrifice less than 10 percent of the hours in a week. (In fact, it's even a bit shy of 9 percent!) The rule? **Study three hours per night, five days per week.**

STUDY: TECHNIQUES AND
TRICKS OF THE TRADE

A student at Tufts basically gave me a verbal tour through all the enhancements and distractions relative to study. He told me that he stays away from Facebook, does listen to music (provided it's not through a headphone), and, most importantly, seeks a private room somewhere on campus. It might be a vacant, isolated classroom or a reading room on the upper floors of the library, but it's got to be private, away from people and other distractions. Hopefully, you'll be able to identify some approaches in this chapter that will work for you.

Patterns

A student from UC Berkeley observed that patterns are key, especially during the first three weeks of school. He said,

> With me it just seems that however I start off is how I continue. Therefore, if I can be intentional about studying during the first couple of weeks, I will tend to stay with that during the rest of the semester. If I start off more lackadaisical, that's how I act. Therefore, the key is to get off to a good start in the first couple of weeks.

Take Your Time

A Hampshire College student said,

> I give myself a lot of time. After I got to college, I soon found that things take me one-and-a-half to two times as long as I had planned. I can't say that I was happy to learn this, but I eventually came to accept the fact that that's just the way it is. I work slowly, and I tend to think a lot about what I do. College happens to be a place that provides me with a lot of time. So I use it.

Semester-at-a-Glance

A St. Lawrence University graduate told me that she was engaged in a work-study program that required her to keep track of her hours, week-to-week, month-to-month on standard employee time cards. She simply grabbed two sets of time cards, got her syllabus out, and marked when items were due and posted them on her wall. Some might think that this approach makes college seem like a job, but when you think about it, if you are enrolled as a full-time college student, then that *is* your job. Think about it this way: Do your job well, and chances are good that you will wind up with a job that you really like later in life.

A student at Southern Methodist University noted that he had a Semester-at-a-Glance calendar that he would update every Sunday night for the new week ahead. He also added that he always had one cup of coffee after dinner but would hold at that in order to be able to sleep later that night.

College-as-a-Job

Speaking of college-as-a-job, a recent Colgate University graduate made no bones about it. She said, "Hey, it's *definitely* a job!" She reasoned that had she not gone to college she would have likely been employed in a 9-to-5 job. Therefore, she decided to make *college* her 9-to-5 job, and she committed to devoting those hours exclusively to academic study: She was either attending class or studying. This caused her to honor the three hours per day of study and left her free at 5:00 PM to do whatever she wanted to do. If you could commit yourself to this process, it strikes me as a real winner.

A Colby College grad echoed the college-as-a-job idea:

One year I had a schedule with no classes on Thursdays and Fridays. Rather than start my weekends on Wednesday nights, I studied from 9 to 5 on those free days. Not only did I then enjoy guilt-free weekends, my whole semester was stress-free, seven days a week.

Unfindable

More than a few students told me that the key word for them was to be "unfindable." Definition: Pick a spot on campus, maybe in the library, and do not tell your friends where you are going. Then seclude yourself, thereby making yourself unfindable.

Lockdown

Taking a similar approach, a Lawrence University student puts himself on "lockdown"; he forces himself to pick a secluded spot in the library and stay away from people. This bears consideration as you will find that, while it may hold an incredible volume of books, a college library is often a social center. Some students delude themselves into thinking that because they are in the library, they are studying when, in fact, they may be doing little more than spending hours standing in the lobby talking with friends or hanging out in the periodical section doing Sudoku puzzles and reading the comics.

Anti-Productivity Zone

A recent Hobart graduate had two things to say. When I asked him about study, he replied with the famous real-estate maxim, "Location, location, location." He believed that location was far more important than the time of day relative to study. He also came down hard on the side of "get out of my room," calling his room an "anti-productivity zone."

Similarly, a Hampshire student observed, "My room turns into a projection of my mind." Sensing my puzzlement, he went on to explain that once he enters his room, he tends to dwell on whatever thoughts are in his head at the time. Therefore, if he needs to engage in more objective scholarly analysis, "I need to be sure that I'm *not* in my room."

Choice of Chinese

A recent Yale graduate told me that her very choice to focus on Chinese forced her to learn how to study. She observed, "American education teaches kids to use natural intelligence and wit but not necessarily how to study. In high school, I never studied, and I got great grades. Then I took Chinese which can really *only* be learned with a great deal of rote and memorization, and rote and memorization can only come from, well, study."

She had to study five days a week because she had a quiz every day. This was particularly challenging because, having taken introductory Chinese courses in high school, she began with Yale's advanced courses. She discovered that the studying she did in Chinese not only helped her in that course, it had the bonus of transferring effective habits and techniques over to all of her other classes. She believes that she did well in them because of the regimen she established in Chinese.

Library

When I asked students to assess the value of the library as a location for study, opinions were all over the park.

A recent grad from William & Mary told me, "I didn't get an effective system down until senior year and that can be summarized in one word: *library.* I just started spending all my time there. I even watched movies there!" He found that moving his base of operations from his room or the campus coffee shop over to the library enhanced his academic performance in a comprehensive way.

A Furman student counters, "Libraries freak me out. They're so silent they're disarming."

A Colby graduate told me that he would study in the library, "but only upstairs." He also noted that his studies took a big step forward in his junior year when he moved into a single room. After that, he abandoned the library, finding that he could effectively study in his room.

A Notre Dame student said he went to the library and sought out the top floor where it was completely silent and no one went.

A Hobart grad swore by the study cubes, or carrels, that he was able to reserve in the library.

Basement Means Business

A Vassar graduate told me that there was a saying at her school: "Basement means business." This referred to the library, she explained. While the main floor of the library tended to be a gathering spot where there was as much if not more socialization than studying, the basement was the place you went if you were serious about doing your work.

A University of New Hampshire student concurred: "There is something productive about going into a room with no clocks and no windows."

Most of the students I spoke with referred to study rituals that had to do with timing and location. One had a simple rule: "Leave my room." There was so much going on in the dorm that she didn't even try to study there and instead considered it a place meant for social interaction while studying was something that was done elsewhere.

Private Study Carrels

Many college libraries offer the opportunity to have a private study carrel, a place where you can keep your books and study. Check to see if one is available at your college.

Music: A Second Look

A surprising number of students told me that they had developed various study playlists for quiet listening through their MP3 players. At first this struck me as counterproductive as my "old school" upbringing taught me to avoid music at study hours. However, the students I spoke with all seemed to be steadfast in their belief in the value of music as a study aid. It made more sense to me when most told me that they tended to find instrumental music more conducive as they were less likely to be distracted by the words. Looking back I have to admit that I can remember listening to quiet jazz when I was studying in school. So that might be an idea to try; however, I would have some system in place to monitor whether you are truly getting work done or whether you are just grooving to the tunes.

Teach to Learn

The Furman student also told me that nothing was more effective in helping her commit information to memory than attempting to teach it to other students. She said, "When I explain to others what I have learned, I learn it better. I'm an auditory learner and, for me, 'out loud' is better."

Several students concurred with the Furman student, indicating that the very act of attempting to explain information to others can help with both understanding and retention. (However, if you go that route, here's a tip: In the event that the objects of your teaching don't thank you for enlightening them, be sure to at least thank them for listening.)

Isolation vs. Group Study

A recent Washington & Lee graduate spoke highly of his group study experience: "Group study was huge! In exchanging information and ideas with others, I always discovered some pertinent points that I had missed from class or in the reading." His reasoning makes sense: "If you only study by yourself, you won't know what you're missing . . . literally."

Similarly, the Washington & Lee grad said, "Peer editing of papers helped me a lot." When he said that, I couldn't help but remember back to my own first year of college when the luck of the draw gave me a roommate who helped me tremendously in editing my papers. As I recall, it took me a little while to put my pride aside and ask for help, but once I did, my writing improved substantially.

Technology

When it comes to technology in all its tools and forms, an NYU student simply said, "Put it away. It's a major time-waster."

A Springfield College student agreed, "Put the phone down and step away from the computer." She told me that she tries to limit herself to books, notebooks, and a pen when it's time to study.

Off-Campus

A graduate from Boston College told me that she tried several locations around campus but found that she got the most done when she retreated to an off-campus coffee shop where she "didn't know anyone."

Similarly, a University of North Carolina (UNC), Greensboro, student echoed the off-campus coffee shop method but added another stipulation: "One that doesn't have Internet access!"

Play Harder Than You Work

The UNC Greensboro student offered up another guideline that is definitely worth consideration: "I don't play harder than I work." He reasoned, "In addition to affording me better grades, following this mind-set also gives me peace of mind should I find myself at a Wednesday night party. When everyone there is saying that they should be at the library instead, I just enjoy myself . . . and guilt-free, I might add."

The Boston College student also added two other provisos to her routine: "I could never wear sweats, and I was in trouble if I tried to read while sitting (to say nothing of lying!) on my bed. I found that I concentrated a lot better if I wore neat clothes and sat upright in a chair."

Typing a Weekly Notes Summary

A graduate of Lynchburg College told me that at the end of each week she would gather her notebooks from each of her classes and type them all up. That way if there was a gap in her understanding or in her notes, she would be able to identify it right away and then confer with a classmate whom she knew to be responsible. This method enabled her to update her understanding each and every week, and it also allowed her to remain calm during the most hectic time of each semester: the week before finals when many of her classmates were scrambling around trying to gather information they had missed during classes they might have failed to attend or during which they had taken shoddy notes. Instead, she found that she was focused solely on internalizing all the information she had already recorded in her notes. It's a much better way to prepare for finals.

"RIP THE GUTS" OUT OF ANY BOOK IN TWO HOURS

One point that I found regularly repeated by college students was the importance of accepting the notion that you'll "never get it all done." Professors typically assign more reading than you will be able to finish. Rather than agonize over the mountain of work to be done, instead just plug into that 3 by 5 rule and keep working. You will find that you will get most of it done and that you'll get better at determining what work applies to the essence of the course.

During my own college days, one of the most important assignments I had came in a history class on historians. Staring me in the face was a big, fat book of 600+ pages titled *The Contours of American History* (1961) by historian William Appleton Williams. My classmates faced books of similar heft and length. The professor told us that we were on our honor to read the entire book in two hours. All of us gawked at him in utter disbelief. There was no way any of us could come close to reading such a book in two hours! The professor pierced our anguished self-pity with a simple statement: "You should be able to rip the guts out of *any* book in two hours. If you can't, then you probably shouldn't be at this school."

Taking his statement as a dare, we set to work. The assignment called for us to write a one-page paper summarizing the essence of the book. In the months that followed we would read our respective books thoroughly in their entirety and would be charged with becoming experts on the author, giving an oral presentation, and writing a ten-page research paper. At the end of the course, we would then compare our initial one-page paper with the longer, fuller version to see how closely the two would be aligned. While it was thirty-five years ago, I can remember all of us being quite surprised to discover that our one-page papers were essentially the same as our ten-page papers minus the detail.

After that exercise I began reading books that way. I would spend an hour or two with the full book reading the chapter headings, the bold print, and the opening and closing paragraphs of each chapter. One of the important lessons about studying is simply the fact that you eventually become better at focusing your efforts. That focus only comes with practice. A good way to practice is three hours per day, five days per week.

WHEN FIFTEEN ISN'T ENOUGH: OFFICE HOURS

During my interviews, a Bowdoin College student frankly told me, "Office hours are the difference between an A and a B student." As tempting as it might be to offer a commentary on that statement, I think it is best just to let it stand on its own. Suffice it to say that going from a B to an A will generally require you to go the extra mile, and going from attending class to a pattern of visiting your professor during office hours represents the same.

Regular Visits

A student at a larger university told me that she made it a practice to drop in on each of her professors during office hours twice a month. While she already had near-perfect class attendance and studied hard, she found that nothing but good came from getting to know the professor; learning what was on the professor's mind; giving consideration to all that came up in lectures, books, and classes; and synthesizing those things with the help of the professor. She claimed it really helped come exam time.

MY STORY

I conclude Rule #2 with a story about my own college days. I tended to be drawn toward theoretical subjects like history, sociology, and religion. I avoided the maths and the sciences. One year I took an economics course where I struggled mightily. I was fine when we were talking about ideas like supply and demand, but when things turned to accounting and other mathematical concepts, I was lost.

A month into the course, I found myself over my head and sinking fast. I had failed the midterm and most of the quizzes. Fearing that I would flunk the course, I adopted an approach that felt shameless: I decided that I would go see the professor every time he had office hours. I repeatedly appeared at his door with my textbook thoroughly underlined with a lot of notes in the margin. He knew I was going to class, and I suppose I was desperately trying to prove to him that I was working hard. (It also dawned on me that it would be one thing to be failing and not working, but to be failing and working hard proved that maybe I really was stupid!) In any case, I just continued what sometimes felt like a desperate strategy.

I came home for Christmas break and announced to my parents that I had most certainly failed economics. (There was no way that the numbers added up to a pass.) When I returned for the second semester, I received my grades and was shocked to discover that I had passed the course! For a while, I avoided the professor because I was actually afraid that he might realize he had made a mistake! At one point, I did see him around campus and mumbled something about my appreciation for all of the extra time he had given me. While he didn't come right out and say it, the message I got went something like this: "Malcolm, if you agree never to take another course in this department, I'll pass you." Whether or not he meant it that way, my experience taught me the importance of showing up, even if it is sometimes a bit hat-in-hand.

DO THE MATH

Let's revisit the math. You'll recall that after you've attended all your classes, your 168-hour week is reduced to 156. Your study time of 15 hours per week knocks things down to 141. That's a lot of time and "idle hands are the devil's workshop." Let's deal with that now. On to Rule #3.

"I see that, in college, you got along equally well with the jocks and the stoners."

3

Rule #3:
(Don't Just Sit There)
Commit to Something

> "It may be the devil.
> It may be the Lord.
> But you're gonna have to serve somebody."
>
> —Bob Dylan

The moments immediately following high school graduation are ones of pure elation and bliss. As a teacher, I find myself weaving through the crowd and trying to find words that will do justice to the bittersweet combination of congratulations and farewell. More than a few times, a particular dialogue has repeated itself.

Amid the back-slapping, hugs, and handshakes immediately following the ceremony, I encounter some of my former athletes with their parents in tow. For a teacher, it's a great feeling when students and their parents express their appreciation. Then it sometimes turns awkward. I ask about intentions regarding college sports: "So, Johnny, are you going to give college lacrosse a shot?" At that point, Mom interjects, "Johnny's not going to go out for lacrosse the first year. He's going to focus on his studies."

Uh-oh. . . . I'm not sure what to say. On the one hand, I don't want to break the mood. On the other hand, here's what I'd like to say to both Johnny and Mom: "Didn't you learn *anything* at school? I mean, did you miss the whole point?"

As Johnny strives to avoid drowning in the ocean of free time that college offers, there are two chances of him using all that extra time for his studies: (1) slim, (2) none. What Johnny and his mother fail to realize is that one of the reasons Johnny excelled at our school was due to a very old adage: "Idle hands are the devil's workshop."

We keep the kids so busy that they don't have time to get into a lot of things they shouldn't get into. As another old adage says, "If you need something done, ask a busy person." Therefore, I say, do the very same thing in college: Make yourself so busy that you don't have time to get into things you shouldn't get into. The wonderful thing about college is that now *you* get to choose whatever it is you want to get busy about.

Here are just a few of the things you can choose:

- trying out for an athletic team
- joining Habitat for Humanity
- trying out for a part in the play
- writing for the newspaper
- getting involved with a campus religious organization
- joining a political campaign
- volunteering in the campus recycling program

Whatever you choose, make it something that requires a regular (preferably daily) commitment. You might even wind up with a "two-fer" and do something that will look good on your future job résumé.

Rule #3 reminds me of an old Bob Dylan song "Gotta Serve Somebody" (1979). While Dylan had a short-lived tenure as a student at the University of Minnesota, his reasoning applies. You will not remain an island unto yourself. *You're gonna serve somebody.* It might be the soccer team. It might be the cast in the play. It might be the newspaper staff. However, it might even be the perpetual party crowd in any and all of its many forms. Not only does this group feature open enrollment with no obligations, its membership typically consists of those who are clueless to the fact that they are, in fact, even members! Sometimes they don't even discover that they're members until they get the pink slip informing them that they have flunked out! So, if you're gonna have to serve somebody, you might as well choose consciously and choose wisely.

A wise choice can be anything that adds to rather than detracts from your well-being as a college student in good standing.

For some folks, especially parents, the idea behind "Commit to Something" might seem counterintuitive. After all, logically speaking, time spent on recreational or extracurricular pursuits is time spent away from academic ones. While I have always subscribed to the notion that a state of busyness is the most productive one for a college student, for the purposes of this book, I decided to suspend my judgment and go out and ask college students for their opinions. So, I asked the same two questions of every current or recent college student who would talk to me:

1. Have you committed to anything extracurricular in college?

2. If yes, how has this commitment enhanced or detracted from your academic progress?

I quickly discovered that most students do, in fact, commit to something and many continue to engage in timeless tried-and-true activities like sports, drama, student journalism, and campus politics. I also discovered a whole new world of fascinating nontraditional activities.

For some students, this can be as simple as a regular, committed regimen of running and weight-training, "regular" and "committed" being the operative words. However, a potential problem with this type of routine is the fact that it lacks accountability to another person or a group. That's fine if you're a self-starter, but it can be less than productive if you're not. In other words, this approach has great potential to lead you to bullshit thyself.

One of the great things about college life is that it allows for the regular to be very irregular. As an example, a William & Mary grad told me that his routine often found him going for long runs at 2:00 or 3:00 AM. (While refraining from judgment on this practice, I'll just say that college may well be the only lifestyle where this approach would have so much as a prayer's chance of working!)

HIGH SCHOOL WITHOUT RULES?

Rule #3 presents a tough message for kids who fantasize about college as a utopia of greener grass, a place that is less structured (maybe even devoid of structure!) with unlimited options. Those who view college as "high school without rules" can be in for a rough go, one that can be avoided without sacrificing too much. You will do well to accept that your life in the future, well beyond college, will be highly structured. Some of that structure is likely to include:

- a career featuring a demanding job
- a marriage
- children
- car loans
- a mortgage
- income taxes

Not only is that the short list, I guarantee you that those things demand much more than twenty-seven hours per week!

MY SOMEBODY

I played lacrosse, a spring sport, in college. I generally did better academic work in the spring than I did in the fall. On any given college weekend, opportunities would present themselves to cut out Thursday afternoon for a ski trip to Sugarloaf or a road trip to Boston with plans to return Monday night, thereby skipping two days of classes. In the fall, I tended to go on such junkets. In the spring, I was unable to go because I had to go to lacrosse practice. This helped keep me focused on the straight and narrow. Not only that, but when our grades slipped, my teammates and I always knew that our coach would think nothing of hauling us into his office and setting us straight. (Come to think of it, he viewed his sport the way that a lot of our professors viewed their subjects.)

HOW TO SERVE SOMEBODY OR SOMETHING

I did not speak with a single college student or recent graduate who didn't place great value on participation in extracurricular activities in college as a source of personal growth and enrichment. After they spoke glowingly of their experiences, I would then ask them to pinpoint the impact of these activities on their *academic* performance. While many had not thought of these activities in that way, I don't think I spoke with any who felt that these activities detracted from their academic performance.

Furthermore, I've spoken with countless adults who found that these extracurricular activities created critical pathways to career choices and professional success in their later lives. For example, lifelong friendships are forged on college athletic teams which lead to professional advancement. I know a college that maintains an alumni lacrosse website where players of all eras can meet, network, and share ideas. I gather that many a job interview and placement have resulted from this affiliation. Having played college sports myself, I can attest to the idea that all of us who played together tend to look out for each other in our later lives, and our professional and personal lives are enhanced by these relationships.

A FEW EXAMPLES

Getting Cut from the Team as a Springboard

One young man went off to Hobart College to play football, made the team as a freshman, but found himself cut as a sophomore. Discouraged, he went to the fall club fair (an event held on many college campuses where extracurricular activities display their opportunities) in hopes of finding a productive way to spend his free time. He wound up getting involved in the campus "Greens" and playing on the college rugby team. Both of these activities helped him maintain a strong mind and a sound body. His work with the Greens also enhanced his studies in political science.

Take the Initiative

A University of Maine graduate told me that he played club lacrosse and also got involved with a student advisory board that ultimately pulled him into a more academic group of people which in turn led to preoccupation with his studies and ultimately a better academic record. He noted that no one recruited him for these clubs; he simply approached these groups and inquired about being involved. The lesson there: Don't wait for others to approach you; take the initiative, and good things will happen.

Opportunities beyond the "Ivory Tower"

Another recent college graduate noted that she got involved with the Philosophy Club which assisted her academic performance. She complemented this by singing in a gospel choir at a local church which she said greatly enriched her experience because it got her out of the "ivory tower" of the campus and caused her to interact with local people whom she never would have met otherwise.

Resident Advisor

One student described her experiences as a resident advisor (RA). At first she was concerned that this would detract from her studies, but she wound up finding that it boosted them. She was expected to be in her dorm room (the best room in the dorm, another RA perk!), and she did a fair amount of tutoring for underclassmen which not only helped them but contributed to her own academic sharpness. Her explanation bears out something I have continually observed as a teacher: Sometimes the best way to be responsible for yourself is to accept responsibility for someone else.

This same young woman told me that the RAs were required to work alumni weekend. While she initially approached this expectation with dread, she wound up having several meaningful discussions with alumni and enhancing her professional network for potential job opportunities.

Some Bowdoin College students serving as RAs told me of a program where they worked with underclassmen in mid-semester to help them set their course schedules for the following semester. At first they thought they were merely providing a helpful service to some younger students, and that made them feel good. However, as the program continued, they found themselves thinking more and more about their own classes. They wound up basically establishing their course schedules before the mad rush later in the semester when their upper classmen peers were doing the same. Hence, their involvement in this program was mutually beneficial.

Sponsor a Family

A Bowdoin College student told me that she was involved in an organization called Sponsor a Family which sometimes called upon her to speak on behalf of the organization to other campus groups as well as to off-campus organizations. On the one hand, these presentations began to feel a bit routine. On the other, she found that it only enhanced her class participation as well as the presentations she had to make in them. She observed, "While I don't know if it made me a better speaker or not, it definitely helped enhance my frame of mind and confidence in making presentations." I'll bet you anything that it did, in fact, help.

Team Sports

As already mentioned, the young man who had to go to early morning hockey practice found that he missed very few classes during the hockey season. One woman who played lacrosse told me that this encouraged a sense of discipline in her life. She traveled a fair amount during the season and had to organize her time, which her coach helped her do.

For me, it was encouraging to speak with so many college students and graduates who derived so much benefit from their own experiences on athletic teams. More examples:

- A Colby grad told me that soccer gave him an immediate "friend group."
- A Tufts lacrosse player experienced the thrill of a national championship, the first his school had ever accomplished in any sport.
- A Furman student said simply, "Club lacrosse allowed me to get my fury out."
- A Washington & Lee wrestler spoke of the sense of order and organization that team membership gave him.

- A student at UC Berkeley was the captain and president of his club lacrosse team. He called that experience the "metronome of my college experience." (I can't say for sure that I know what that means, but it sure sounds like a good thing.)

A recent Kenyon College grad held her experience on the basketball team in a similar light. In addition to the thrill of competition, she served on a student committee of campus athletes representing each team on campus. Representing his or her respective team, each member of the committee would select a game on the upcoming schedule that every other Kenyon athlete would be highly encouraged (read: "required!") to attend. That way, every team on campus from the highly popular to the more obscure would get the chance to play in front of a capacity crowd. It was great for school spirit and a lot of fun.

Team Sports in Perspective

At the same time, some student-athletes warned of the importance of keeping sports in perspective. A Boston College basketball player told me that she opted not to play her senior year. While a whole new world opened up that had been obscured by her 24-7 commitment to basketball, she acknowledged that her grades were not as strong after she left the team: "I finished OK, but didn't do as well."

At the same time, her decision also led to some great opportunities. Combined with her choice to major in communications, her involvement with the Boston College Council of Women caused her to connect with a Boston radio personality which, in turn, led to a job with ESPN where she served as an international reporter for the World Series. After the Series ended, she got a chance to do statistics and production work with the Boston Revolution pro soccer team. In short, her time on the basketball team helped open up these doors; her decision not to play that final year gave her the time to take advantage of them.

A Washington College student valued his three years on the varsity lacrosse team but felt that his decision not to play his senior year was one of the best decisions he made in college because it allowed him to turn his attentions to the job market and prepare for the next phase of his life. "Funny," I said to him, "but it sounds like it was important for you to stay with it in the early going and that it was also important for you to drop it after you had given it the old college try, so to speak." While I don't know if he had ever heard the expression the "old college try," he replied, "Definitely." In any case, this young man's experience shows that even though it may not seem like it while you're reading this book, college does indeed eventually end.

Toward this end, the Washington College student's eyes lit up when he told me about a project he was involved in during his final year at school. As juniors, he and a friend took a stab at music promotion and organized a music festival on campus. Noting that the experience earned him more knowledge than dollars, he and his partner were gearing up for a larger off-campus outdoor production that would feature at least one national act and would target a larger audience while maintaining the college crowd as a base. As a business major, he had taken many courses that proved helpful to his vision, but this activity gave him the chance to put all that learning into practice.

A Lynchburg College graduate noted that she ran cross-country her freshman year and decided not to do it the following year. She discovered she wound up with too much time on her hands and really did not rebound until her junior year. The moral of the story might be that if you are engaged in something on a regular basis in the early going and then decide later to stop doing that thing (whatever it is), you would be wise to plan on the fact that you may need to fill this time with something else productive in order to maintain the quality of your performance as a student.

Student Government

Several students spoke of the residual benefits of getting involved in student government. A Hobart grad told me that after getting cut from the football team, he turned his attention to the Campus Greens movement, a natural match with his major in environmental studies.

A Colby grad initially didn't give it much thought before agreeing to serve as president of his dormitory. Then he realized that the position came with a choice room in the dorm and that's pretty much the gold standard for college students. His responsibilities in this position also included regular meetings with the president of the college and other senior administrators which served to demystify the inner workings of the college.

Similarly, a Bowdoin College student sponsored an open house in his dormitory. Several faculty came including an administrator at the school's Career Center. This young man got to know the Career Center representative and established a contact that he believes will be useful "when I'm spending more and more time at the Career Center during the latter part of my college career." Again, this is a very simple example of how getting engaged in something can have a residual benefit.

A student at Furman University observed, "My role as president of the College Democrats forced me to tackle my fear of public speaking as I was expected to introduce visiting leaders and speakers. This helped me in terms of classroom participation and overall confidence. I also learned a whole lot about party politics at both the local and national levels."

Bring It with You

One student from NYU engages in what might be considered somewhat unconventional extracurricular activities and somehow manages to effectively combine them with academic study. One of his passions is comedy, and he regularly performs in New York comedy clubs. He has a simple rule with academics: "I bring it with me." When I asked him to elaborate, he replied, "I always have a book or notes with me. If I'm at a comedy club waiting to go on, I sit in a back room reading a book." When I challenged him on the practicality of that, he came back very seriously saying, "It works for me." And he has done well academically so I have to believe him. Again, know thyself.

Ask a Busy Person

A UC Berkeley student definitely subscribes to the time-honored notion: *If you need something done, ask a busy person.* He observed, "If I have seven things to do, I will scurry around

and make sure that they all get done with reasonable time allotted for each. If I have one thing to do, I will put it off until
the last minute and maybe even miss getting it done."

Echoing the recurring theme on the value of staying busy,
a Furman University student observed, "Too much free time,
and I don't get as much done. Not only that, but the more slack
time I have in my schedule, the more my test anxiety increases."

Real World Goes to College

A student from Notre Dame noted that he was in an organization called the Student International Business Club. They
developed a project for Price Waterhouse accountants, and he
and a half dozen of his peers traveled to Chicago to make the
presentation. He described it to me as a "three-fer":

1. They got to meet some of the principals at a major Price
   Waterhouse office.
2. They had a great time.
3. They learned a great deal about the whole world of
   accounting which is their professional ambition after
   college.

As he said, "We did a 'real world' thing with a real company,
and that was truly exciting given our majors in college."

Similarly, a Southern Methodist University student told me
that he is in a club called the Scholars Club that brings academic speakers to campus and which has enhanced his academic performance in several ways. He is also the academic
chair of his fraternity and once a month he is responsible for
inviting a teacher to dinner. Each month he gets to know that
particular professor on a personal basis which also can only
help him on a number of fronts.

Get a Job!

A student from Tufts stressed the value of a work-study job. He needed to do it for the extra money and noted that the vast majority of work-study jobs allow you to study. As a result, he often found himself manning a desk where there were few passersby. He got a lot of work done, and he also earned spending money to boot. As the saying goes, *Good work if you can get it*—especially from a studying standpoint.

A UNC Greensboro student told me about his job supervising private birthday parties for young children. It was fun, and he earned spending money to show for it.

A William & Mary grad initially took a work-study job tutoring student-athletes for the extra spending money. However, he ultimately derived two benefits from the experience which he had not previously considered. For one, he found that it enhanced his own understanding of his own academic work. For another, it proved to be excellent training for the line of work he chose after graduation: teaching.

Theater

A recent Yale graduate told me that she got involved with an experimental theater troupe called The Control Group which she joined during her first year. She notes, "They were my family; we created an original play every term, and it was truly an exercise in following through as the topics tended to be totally random: dreams, religion, Communism, etc. It was almost like taking another class."

Offering an example of her efforts in The Control Group, she observed that a regular technique was to create a sixty-second piece of theater. Participants might be given a piece of rope, a clipboard, and a poem, and would then be expected to improvise a sixty-second piece of performance art and perform it in front of the group. She described the experience as something that demanded "fearless creativity," and it contributed mightily to the rest of her college experience.

On the one hand, you might wonder how an exercise like this could possibly contribute to one's academic progress, but first consider what it might take to prepare and present that sixty-second piece of improv theater in front of an audience. Then once you get that into your head, just think how easy it would then be to participate in discussions in any of your other classes—truly a piece of cake.

Big Brother/Sister

A student at Bowdoin College told me of the benefits he has experienced as a Big Brother to a student at a local middle school. While he has come to develop a genuine bond with this young man, he says it helps him because "I don't want to be a hypocrite. There is no way I want to be caught telling this young man that he needs to buckle down and do his homework if I'm not doing the same myself." He has found the direct correlation between how much he encourages his Little Brother and how hard he works himself. Again we see that sometimes the best way to be responsible for yourself is to be responsible for someone else.

A recent Colby grad told me that she was involved in an organization called Colby Cares About Kids, a big sister program where she met twice weekly with a local elementary school student. While you might think that such a commitment could potentially detract from academic study time, this woman reasons that it challenged her sense of time management, forcing her to be aware of when papers and tests were

due so she would still be able to honor her mentoring responsibilities. Again, this is another case of having more things to
do and ending up more organized as a result.

Shake and Bake

My discussions uncovered a range of extracurricular opportunities that I never could have imagined. Here's one of my
favorite ones: A student at Hampshire College enthusiastically
told me about his association with a group called Shake and
Bake where participants bring their own baked goods to meetings and share their culinary results while simultaneously dis-
cussing . . . Shakespeare. At first I thought he was putting me
on, but he clearly wasn't. He was also obviously very into the
whole thing! (If nothing else, it certainly shows that the Bard is
indeed timeless and even appetizing.) As he said, "I not only
learned how to bake a whole bunch of new things, I learned a
lot of Shakespeare." Hey, mission accomplished!

Residual Benefit

If I had to identify a theme of my conversations and interviews with college students relative to the value of "Commit
to Something," it would be the notion of residual benefit.
Most students found that as a result of throwing themselves
into something, they felt better about themselves *and* invariably received unexpected benefits as a bonus. As an example, a Bowdoin College student told me that he got involved
with an altruistic organization called The Common Good
which strives to support a range of individuals and groups
off-campus. It just so happens that one of the supervisors
was a native Spanish speaker, and so the student began to

have his daily conversational interactions with her in Spanish. He later found that his Spanish grade improved, a result of what he professes was a direct link between these conversations and his grade.

Regrets

A Hobart student told me that he regretted the fact that he didn't do more in the extracurricular realm. He noted that he took his courses, got to know his professors as friendly acquaintances, and graduated with a solid GPA, but he felt he missed out by not getting more involved in pursuing some of his interests outside class. He urged other students to take advantage of whatever was available to them.

A WORD ABOUT GREEK LIFE

In my career, I have tended to steer college-bound students away from fraternity and sorority life. Perhaps I've been influenced by popular notions of fraternities as they have been portrayed in movies like *Animal House* and *Old School*. Perhaps this is also due to the all-too-many students I have known who have taken a turn for the worse once they joined a fraternity. However, many of my discussions during the research for this book have perhaps shed a new light on the subject and helped me see new possibilities in the Greek life. I gather that fraternities on many campuses have changed substantially since my own undergraduate days.

My alma mater has prohibited fraternities as have many liberal arts colleges, especially those in the Northeast. Hence, I surmise that fraternities have changed in order to maintain their survival. In any case, a student at the University of New Hampshire told me that his fraternity had a mandatory study hall for pledges. Once you went beyond the pledge period and were a full-fledged member, you were allowed to make these decisions on your own, but he felt that a mandatory study hall in his early going truly helped his initial transition to college. So, if you plan to go Greek, join a fraternity that is going to demand the best out of you.

A Washington & Lee grad expressed genuine gratitude for the benefits he derived from frat life: "By nature, I tended to be introverted in college. Joining a fraternity enabled me to get closer with a group of people than I otherwise would not have. We were all thrown together, got along, and helped each other out. It was a positive influence for me."

A William & Mary grad counters this praise, "For me, living in a fraternity was a horrible mistake. It negatively impacted my academics and actually turned me antisocial before it was over. It may work for some, but the whole thing turned out to be a major regret of mine."

WHERE'S THE KRYPTONITE?

As powerful as Superman is, there is one thing that can completely bring him to his knees: Kryptonite. Superman must always be on guard as any exposure to Kryptonite will render him weak and ineffective. So I ask you—what is *your* Kryptonite? Do you know where it is? Do you have an effective Kryptonite detector that is fully charged and in optimal working order?

When I was eighteen years old, my Kryptonite was the party life. I was drawn to it. Looking back, I undoubtedly would have performed much better in college had I not been so engaged in that part of it. I made plenty of stupid decisions and bad moves because of it.

However, as I look back on my college years, maybe the best decision I made is owed to my Kryptonite detector. Here's the story:

When I arrived in college, I fancied myself a lacrosse player with an eye out for a good time. We freshmen were rushed by all of the fraternities on campus. While my alma mater doesn't even have fraternities anymore, they were a big part of the social life when I was there. For me it was really a question of not "if," but which one.

On the very first night, I received a bid (an offer) to join one fraternity that really seemed to me to be where everything was happening. A lot of the lacrosse players were members. They really knew how to throw a party, and I really liked all the members. During Rush Week, I received some bids from some other houses as well, but I spent probably 80 percent of my time at that first one. When Rush Week ended, we were expected to make our selection at dinner. I began walking down the stairs from my dorm on my way over to the fraternity for dinner and was looking forward to it. I started walking across the campus quad, and something stopped me in my tracks.

It was as though Jiminy Cricket was sitting on my right shoulder saying, "Malcolm, what, are you kidding me? You can't join that fraternity. Guys are going to be going out every night of the week and, guess what, you will be tagging along with them because you don't have the self-discipline not to. You need to join that other fraternity (Deke) instead. It will be better suited to the actual current state of your self-discipline (or lack thereof!)."

While, I don't know what possessed me, I did do an about-face, walked in the other direction on the quad, and accepted the bid to join Deke. I liked the Deke house, but I was not as excited about joining it. I sensed that the house had an ethic that went something like this: "We party hard on the weekends, but we study during the week. If you plan to party during the week, take it outside."

Without my Kryptonite detector, I would have likely said, *I'm eighteen. I'm a high school graduate. I can vote. I'm an adult. I'm going to prove that I have self-discipline, join the fraternity I want to join, and rise above it all.*

Had my Kryptonite detector read "false positive," it might have led me to justify that position. However, it seemed to be working on that particular day, and the message I got was, *Malcolm, face the fact that your self-discipline is underdeveloped at this point in time. So don't needlessly put yourself in a circumstance where you have to exhibit so much of it.*

That was the wisest decision I made in college. It's quite possible that I could have joined that first house and everything would have worked out fine. As it turned out, I certainly discovered that pockets of people at the Deke house did indeed party on weeknights, and I managed to find them in rather short order. I also came to find that plenty of guys at the other house studied during the week. (My hunch is that I would *not* have found them . . .)

At the same time, I did get through that first year, and it taught me something about myself: If I place myself around motivated people, I am more likely to respond in kind. If I place myself among people who want to have a good time, I'm more likely to . . . respond in kind. While I think I have improved my self-discipline, I would also tell you that forty years later much of that is still true.

My fraternity experience taught me the importance of having a functioning Kryptonite detector. I ask you to make sure that you have one, and one of the best ways to do that is to ask other people if they think you have one. (And, yes, this does include your parents.) In the meantime, the best substitute for an effective Kryptonite detector is to follow Rule #3 and "Commit to Something."

NO REGRETS?

I'm always puzzled whenever I hear people say, "I have no regrets." When I hear that, I quietly think to myself there must be something wrong with me because I have quite a few. However, I have learned that it's one thing to have regrets about those things that I did do. Those don't bother me as much as the regrets I have over those things that I *wish* I had done. Looking back on college, I don't regret any of the things that I got involved in, but there are plenty that I wished I'd done. I wish I had

- DJ'd my own radio show;
- gone to more art shows;
- gone to more plays;
- taken a shot at the football team;
- been bolder in acting upon my romantic crushes;
- studied harder (especially in the first two years);
- participated more in my classes, etc.

So, when you get to college, jump in with all fours.

MORE MATH: 126

168 – 12 (class) = 156
156 – 15 (study) = 141
141 – 15 (serve) = 126

When we began Rule #3, you had 141 hours to play with (141 = 168 minus 12 for class attendance and then minus 15 for study). Let's say that you honored Rule #3 by committing 2½ hours per day, 6 days per week (15 hours). You're still left with 126 hours to do whatever you want. That's a lot of time. Enjoy, but don't forget to get some sleep!

"For my junior year abroad, I'm going to learn how to party in a foreign country."

4

Rule #4: Get a Mentor

/ "I get by with a little help from my friends."

—The Beatles /

HOME AWAY FROM HOME

In the early 80s, a student of mine headed out to Western Illinois University on an athletic scholarship. I had no doubt that he would do the job on the football field and basketball court. (He's the only student-athlete I've ever taught or coached who went on to play two Division 1 sports.) However, I did worry a bit about how he would fair in the new and unfamiliar circumstances he would encounter. He had grown up in inner-city Washington, DC, and was most comfortable with urban life. As he got off the plane in rural Illinois and observed a vast skyline of haystacks and farm silos,

I doubt he could have fully imagined the sharp cultural and racial shake-up he was about to face. Unpacking his things in his dormitory, I do know that he wondered to himself, *Have I landed on Mars?*

Years later I asked him how he coped with the challenge of the experience. With a smile on his face, he told me the story of how a man who directed the university's photo lab and whose wife worked in the bursar's office had taken an interest in him. Sensing that the young student-athlete might be homesick, the man began inviting him to his home for dinners, sleepovers, and entertainment with his family. He also took him rabbit and deer hunting, activities the student had never so much as pondered let alone actually done before. Before long, the relationship evolved into a home-away-from-home where this student was able to do everything from laundry to watching TV. Mostly it was a haven where he could just sit around and talk.

This new relationship also gave him the chance to make some spending money by working around the house. (The family kept four horses and had vegetable gardens.) Before his time was up there, my young friend confessed that he had actually taken to occasionally wearing a cowboy hat and boots and had even developed a taste for *some* country music—"I even started to like it after a while"—a fact that he kept mostly to himself to avoid being teased mercilessly by his buddies back home in DC. As his athletic eligibility came to its conclusion, something else dawned on him: Unlike a lot of his peers on his basketball and football teams— he was a starter on both teams during his time there—he was able to proudly say, "I'm a student in good standing who is graduating on time."

As he thought back to those days, it became clear to both of us that a big reason for this young man's collegiate success was due to the fact that he had unknowingly created a sense of family that evolved into an effective support system in what had initially seemed like an alien world to him. While his mentor was neither a basketball star nor a scholar, the student's support system enabled him to excel both academically and athletically. And the interesting thing about this is that he just stumbled into it. He originally thought that this relationship was just a pleasant complement to his college experience, something that could help ward off homesickness. He came to realize that it was actually a critical lynchpin to the success he experienced both in the classroom and on the athletic field.

Babysitting Gig

On a more personal level, my wife and I had mixed feelings when our oldest headed off to college 2,000 miles away. While we were very excited by the opportunities that would be available to our daughter at the University of Denver, we also knew that we would miss having her around our home.

Our daughter seemed to buckle down and get to work shortly after she arrived, and that made us feel good. What made us feel even better, however, was the relationship she soon developed with a former student of ours, his wife, and their two young children. Ironically, this former student actually babysat my daughter when she was barely a year old. And here she was, eighteen years later, babysitting his children. This afforded her the chance to earn some extra money, but it also contributed mightily to her success.

When she first arrived in Denver, our daughter did not know a soul. Her babysitting arrangement essentially allowed her to become a part of a new family. In addition to allowing her to earn some spending money, her "bosses" made it possible for her to take advantage of the unique opportunities available in Denver such as hiking in the Rockies, cheering with Bronco fans, or skiing in Aspen.

But more than that, both her mother and I are convinced that this surrogate family relationship was an important contribution to the success our daughter experienced academically at school. While it probably doesn't hurt that both the mother and the father had also studied at the University of Denver, there is no question that this relationship was very important to our daughter on many levels.

During her junior year, my daughter headed off to a semester abroad in London, and it was clear that one of the things she struggled with the most was the idea of breaking away from her new family. In any case, the point of this chapter is that a support system can be a very valuable resource in college, and both my wife and I are convinced that this particular one was especially valuable to our daughter.

Both of these stories serve as examples of how valuable a mentor can be to you as you head off to college. While you will undoubtedly have mentors in your peer group, sometimes there is something about the separation of a generation that can set up a dynamic in which you receive counsel and advice, go off and do it yourself, and then reconvene for more advice and counsel. If you're lucky, you may even develop a lifelong touchstone of friendship and support.

"COME TO THINK OF IT . . ."

During my interviews for this book, I received varied reactions when it came to the mentor question. Some students really could not identify any adult mentors in their college life. Some of the students (or young alums) in this boat regretted the lack of such experience, while others seemed ambivalent. Interestingly, there were also a number of interviewees who initially said that this question did not apply to them and then later in our interview would catch themselves waxing reverently about a professor, a coach, a local merchant, or a campus buildings and grounds staff member who had played some key role in their college experience. In the midst of such explanations, more than a few times I heard some stop in mid-sentence and say, much to their own surprise, "You know, I take that back. Maybe I did have a mentor after all." Funny thing about mentors: Sometimes they creep up on you out of nowhere. Sometimes they've been there all along, and you didn't even know it.

IN PRAISE OF GREAT PROFESSORS— A MAKE-UP CALL

Early in this book, I had some irreverent good-natured fun with some professorial stereotypes. To set the record straight, let it be known that my interviews with college students past and present revealed the incredibly important life-changing role that a great professor can play in a young person's life.

Truth be told, I could probably write a whole new book on the stories I heard. Here are a few.

A Hampshire College student said simply, "I think I'm the only student on campus who has taken three courses from this particular demanding professor of Buddhism and Japanese. This has created a bond between us, and I count him as a valued personal friend in my life."

Several students I spoke with simply noted that it was nice to be on friendly terms with some of their professors. A student from SMU noted that he developed a very good relationship with an English and Sociology professor despite the fact that he didn't major in either subject. Since he had stumbled into this valuable relationship somewhat accidentally, he told me that his experience inspired him to make it a point to go around and introduce himself to all of the professors in his own department regardless of whether he intended to take their courses. It can't hurt.

A student from Hobart College had a similar experience. In fact, he said, "Forming relationships with professors really *made* college for me." One of these was an economics professor, which might have seemed unlikely given the fact that the student only took two such classes during his entire time in college. A major in East-Asian studies, he had a goal to become fluent in Japanese. No matter how good a professor might be in class, it only stands to reason that prospects for fluency are greatly enhanced by one-on-one discussions outside of class, and that's what he did with his professor.

Another Hobart grad said simply, "I found a home in the Department of Environmental Studies. The chair of the department was great. I took all of his classes and always felt as though I could approach him." Sometimes the value of a solid college experience can be as simple as that.

The Notre Dame student was blown away by a priest in his dorm who knew everyone's name in the dorm before school even began: "He walked right up to me out of the blue and called me by name even though he had never laid eyes on anything but a picture that had been presumably in my admissions application. I've had tons of one-on-one conversations with this mentor, and he greatly helped me out." This student also traveled to Australia, and he became close with a professor who also traveled there. The student has since received invaluable guidance as well as recommendations for employment opportunities.

A Furman student spoke of an advisor in the Department of Religion. As valuable as this advisor was to her in and out of class, she noted that a whole new world opened up after she got to know his wife and was welcomed into their home. After getting to know them as husband and wife, she concluded, "Their relationship became a model for the type I would like to have someday with a lifelong partner. Not only that, but I observed that they read a lot and have inspired me to do the same."

A Colby College grad, today a teacher, spoke glowingly of a particular English professor: "I never learned more about myself or the English language as I did with him. Not only that, but he's the standard I strive for as an educator."

He went on to explain, "However, I had to make the first move. It was hard to even get into his classes, and he was very tough, but his demanding approach taught me initiative. I was never quite sure where I stood, but when I graduated he promised me a recommendation. In fact, he said, 'Contact me first.'"

COACHES

Perhaps not surprising, a number of student-athletes spoke of special relationships with coaches. A former basketball player at Kenyon College said,

> I can't honestly say that I "liked" my coach, but I respected her. Early on she helped me decide whether or not I was going to sign on for a four-year commitment to hoops. I decided to do so. Then, junior year there was a shift where she began to expect more leadership out of me, and she taught me how to commit to something wholeheartedly. Throughout my time at Kenyon, she was the mentor who would listen but would not hold your hand.

When I asked the Kenyon grad to pinpoint the essence of what she learned from her coach as a mentor, she replied, "Your personal and professional life, when it comes down to it, is . . . your life. You can't just separate the two at your convenience. In the end, you must operate on all cylinders because everything is connected."

A Washington & Lee grad was grateful for the relationship he had with one of his college wrestling coaches. While the coach gave great instruction on the mat, he and the student also painted houses together one summer and became lifelong friends.

A Boston College grad praised one of her teachers from high school. He taught her math and coached her in basketball. She said, "His dedication and commitment to his students carried right over into college. We often talked on the phone, exchanged e-mails, and he came to a number of my college games. He was definitely a positive force in my *college* experience, and today he is one of my closest friends."

ADVISORS

A recent Yale graduate told me how her advisor had helped her with her writing and much more. She said, "I had not been close to any teachers in high school, and it took me a long time to get comfortable with the idea of adults as friends. I just had never perceived them in that light."

It all started with a C+ on a paper. Not only was this one of her first assigned papers at Yale, it was the worst grade she had ever gotten in school:

> I don't believe I had ever received a C+ before that. I received mostly A's with some B's in high school, and I rarely studied. To add insult to injury, when I initially passed this particular paper in, I felt pretty good about it and assumed that the professor would feel likewise when it came time to give it a grade. Then when the professor passed the paper back and I saw that C+ on the first page, I was crushed. I decided to go see the professor. Not very sympathetic to my plight, my professor frankly said, "You have backed nothing up. This simply is not well written."

The student continued,

> Feeling worse, I considered going to my advisor. At first, I wasn't even sure why this person was my advisor at all. After

all, I was interested in East Asian studies, and my assigned advisor was a French professor who happened to be the advisor for my residence hall. She agreed to see me, took a look at my paper, and said, "I hate to break it to you, but he's right."

By this point, I was ready to listen. I soon saw that what had worked in high school—flowing, opinionated, free-wheeling and long-winded papers—was not going to work in college. I began to take all my papers to my advisor. By demanding that I back all of my opinions up with concrete evidence, my advisor made me a better writer. I had never considered the idea that criticism could be a positive force. In the past, I considered critics to be nothing more than people who didn't like me, and I didn't like them. Although this had been my initial reaction to my advisor, thankfully something made me realize that she was helping me, and it made all the difference.

However, our Yale grad soon learned that the value of this mentoring relationship was not limited to academic improvement:

As time went on, I came to see that my advisor was much more than a critic. I soon discovered, much to my surprise, that she and I played in the university orchestra together. I played the cello, an instrument I had played for several years, and she was a novice viola player. The interesting thing was, in this endeavor, I was better than she was, and she was clearly not inhibited by this fact. She simply continued to muddle along to learn the instrument. It was as though we had reversed roles and her willingness to do so made me respect her and made it much easier to listen to the advice she was giving me.

Consider the fact that our Yale student only went to her advisor because she got a bad grade on a paper. Maybe if she had received a B- she wouldn't have gone to see her at all. In any case, her decision to take the initiative and follow through put her on the road to writing better and markedly improving her grades. Furthermore, it is doubtful that she would have enacted her academic turnaround on her own. She needed the kind of input that could only be provided by a third party. Not only did this input help her upgrade her academic performance, it resulted in a very beneficial relationship with a mentor. All this goes to show that if you go out of your way to initiate interactions with potential adult role models, good things can happen. So don't wait around for them to find you.

BOOSTERS

A student at UC Berkeley told me that some of the parent boosters of his lacrosse team were invaluable to him in many ways. Being a club, the team did not enjoy the perks that traditionally come with varsity status. As president of the club, this student was responsible for organizing everything.

As a result, this young man is not only receiving valuable business training, he has had the opportunity to interact with parents, learn what they do in their professional lives, and essentially network with interesting people while developing a meaningful support system. (This latter attribute comes in especially handy given that his home is 3,000 miles away on the East Coast.)

On a similar note, it has occurred to me that those who play on varsity teams perhaps miss out on a potential opportunity simply because of the very fact that everything is provided for them. My daughter plays a similar role for her club lacrosse team at the University of Denver. When I went out to one of her tournaments in California, it dawned on me that the duties she and her teammates are expected to perform—negotiate the best hotel rates, budget dining costs, arrange travel, arrange for rental cars—is actually serving as training for how to operate a small business. While she might complain that the university ought to be doing more for her club, I'm thinking that the whole thing fits perfectly with her major: Business.

OTHER EXAMPLES

AA Sponsor

A few college students cited adults who served as sponsors in Alcoholics Anonymous. It's hard to imagine a more important mentor than that one.

A Mentor's Intentional Intrusion

A recent graduate of Lynchburg College told me that she did not initially intend to go to college at all. She noted, "No one in my family had ever gone to college, and it did not occur to me that we could afford it." Furthermore, she didn't really see herself as a student and was considering going into the military when she changed her mind at the last minute and wound up at Lynchburg.

Shortly after she got to college she encountered a particular professor in political science. "He had a great personality, and he was also one of the hardest teachers I had ever had. He always 'over-assigned,' meaning he gave you more work than you could do, but he always demanded that you get it done anyway."

"However," she went on to explain,

> One day he also went one step further where he actually approached and confronted me, telling me, "You wear your emotions on your sleeve in your work and in your personal interactions." My first thought was, *Who are you to talk to me like that? I've never had anyone invade my life in that way before.*
>
> I wasn't pleased. I also wondered if my decision to go to college had been the right one. My professor then went on to explain what "wearing your emotions on your sleeve" meant (I wasn't sure), and then set me up to work on a series of projects with students from other colleges where we would assemble in Washington, DC, and conduct mock UN or European Union assemblies. I wound up rising in the ranks of this program, and I totally lost myself in the enthusiasm of it. This ended up giving an incredible boost to my self-esteem. Throughout my school days, I received many athletic awards but had never earned any academic accolades. This was a new feeling, and I liked it. Eventually it dawned on me that the only reason I received these accolades was because this particular professor pushed me into something that I did not initially want to do at all.

Mentors do that sometimes.

Brutal Truths

When we think of the word "mentor," we think of warm feelings for someone who encourages us with praise and support. To be sure, sometimes we need this. However, the Lynchburg grad's story reminds us that sometimes we also need people who will be frank and demanding with us. That was certainly true with me and my coach in college. While I might have wished at the time that he had been a bit more warm and fuzzy, the hindsight of three decades causes me to know that my improvement as a player was in no small part due to his relentless and demanding expectations. This is not to say I was a star, because I was not, but I do think that he helped me get as close to my potential as anyone could have, and therein lies the deepest value of a mentor.

Similarly a Bowdoin College student told me that she was at first intimidated by one professor because this professor had the tendency to offer her suggestions in unvarnished fashion. For example, she would say,

- "You're better than this."
- "Don't act like an idiot."
- "This is bullshit."

When another student in our discussion group chuckled, I said, "I gather you had the same professor." He replied, "Indeed I did. She's great. Super-demanding, but great." As tough as this professor is, both students pointed to her as a key to the success they had experienced.

Ask yourself, *In going to see my professor or advisor, am I motivated by hopes that he or she will make me feel good, or am I going to really try to find "What's Up?"* If you truly want to know what's up, then you need to know what is going well and what is not. If you can get to the point where you can take the advice without taking it personally, you will be taking a great step forward.

Just as college is a step in the direction of a world that can at first seem a bit impersonal or indifferent, the work world you will step into a few years later is even less friendly at the start. Consider the fact that your education is ultimately leading you to a place where performance is all that matters. I walked away from this particular discussion feeling that these two students get that idea. Another way of looking at it: When you go ask someone for help, be ready for anything. You may initially get something that you don't like, but what you get just may turn out to be very helpful down the road and may be exactly what you need.

Keep Your Eyes Open

It has been said that when you're truly ready to learn the lesson, the teacher will emerge. So keep your eyes open for that person who just might help you reach heights that you would not attain on your own. And that's a good thing.

5

Rule #5: "Procrastination Kills"

> "Nothing is so fatiguing as the eternal hanging on of an uncompleted task."
>
> —William James

Some of my interviews for this book involved group sessions with current college students from various schools. Once while wrapping up one of the sessions, I concluded with a simple question: *If you could share a single pearl of wisdom with a student who was entering college tomorrow morning, what would it be?*

I asked the students to think about their answer for a minute or two and then began scanning the room for answers. Before long, a student from Hartwick College raised his hand, pensively paused, grinned, and announced, "Procrastination kills."

As soon as these two words were said, every student in the room chuckled and before long, the room was filled with the chatter of personal tales of procrastination horror stories sprinkled with various tactics of counterattack. Some of these tactics had proven to be effective and others had failed miserably. (As the discussion continued, I began to envision a whole new book—the Sequel???—that could perhaps be titled *College—What* Not *To Do*.)

Yep, at some point you will most certainly come up against the Procrastination Thing. (And I'm not only talking about college. I daresay that it even revisited me while I was writing this book!) In fact, while writing this chapter, I discovered that there are an incredible number of quotes on the subject. Here are a few choice ones:

"Never put off until tomorrow what you can do the day after tomorrow."

—Mark Twain

"Procrastination is opportunity's assassin."

—Victor Kiam

"I do my work at the same time each day: The last minute."

—unknown

"Procrastination is something best put off until tomorrow."

—Gerald Vaughn

"The two rules of procrastination: (1) Do it today. (2) Tomorrow will be today tomorrow."

—unknown

"If you want to make an easy job seem mighty hard, just keep putting off doing it."

—Olin Miller

"Procrastination is the art of keeping up with yesterday."

—Don Marquis

And finally, my personal favorite:

"Anyone can do any amount of work, provided it isn't the work he is supposed to be doing at that moment."

—Robert Benchley

You have to wonder if these folks came up with these gems while they were in the midst of doing battle with their own procrastination. In any case, I also came across a few that offer the plain and simple truth on how to *beat* procrastination:

"To think too long about doing a thing often becomes its undoing."

—Eva Young

"It is an undoubted truth, that the less one has to do, the less time one finds to do it in."

—Earl of Chesterfield

"No matter which remedy you end up using to beat procrastination, you will definitely find that the best way to get something done is to begin."

—unknown

Read on for anecdotes and random solutions from college
students, present and past.

Go Minimalist

A UC Berkeley student offered the ultimate minimalist pre-
scription. As though cutting through the fog, he said, "Just
get it done." In other words, don't make excuses; just sit down
right now wherever you are and do your work!

A Hampshire College student followed suit: "I try to work
almost all the time." Hey, there's something to be said for
keeping it simple.

He went on to explain,

> As a college student I've moved from trying to impress to a
> focus on what I want to learn. This has caused me to let go of
> the idea that there is a specific way that I'm supposed to do
> things or a particular place I'm supposed to be in the grading
> hierarchy or that I'm supposed to be spending my time pleas-
> ing other people. Now I just want to learn, and I regard college
> as a good place to do that. As a result, I find that I don't pro-
> crastinate all that much.

IN PRAISE OF RULES

If you're looking for more specifics, an NYU student said
that he has come to accept that he functions better with rules.
He said,

When I left high school, I wanted nothing to do with rules. So I started off at college with one rule: *No more rules!* It wasn't long before I came to a reluctant realization: Rules are good for me. I perform better with them. So now I make rules. Lots of them. For example:

- If I read this book or write a draft of that paper tonight, I can go out the next two nights.
- If I don't skip class one time this week, I can go to this concert Saturday night.
- If I go to the gym to lift weights three days this week, I will treat myself to a visit to a casino this weekend.

He then concluded simply, "Hey, It works for me."

A Boston College grad adds, "When I wanted to go out on the town and do something special, I would find an announcement of the event in the paper or just draw up some sort of fancy announcement and put it on the wall of my room. Then I'd tell myself that before I could enjoy myself, I had to get my work done."

Plan a Day Early

A student at Springfield College has a fool-proof procedure. She simply places all of her due dates a day early on her calendar. In other words, if a paper is due on Friday the 29th, she will mark it down as being due on Thursday the 28th. She then goes about her daily business as though the dates in her calendar are the actual deadlines and winds up getting everything done with twenty-four hours to spare. (Her system reminds me of my dearly departed father-in-law who always set his watch ten minutes fast. He was never late for anything!)

Eat and Sleep Right

An SMU student simply noted that a well-rounded lifestyle warded off procrastination: "If I get enough sleep, eat right, get exercise, I'll do all right, and if I find that I'm in a phase of procrastinating, chances are good that I'm falling short in one of those areas."

While our Boston College basketball player agreed that her team membership helped ward off the dangers of procrastination, she also stressed the importance of sleep, emphasizing, "If I didn't get sleep, there's no way I could study. In fact, I couldn't get much of anything done, much less function in any meaningful way."

Take a Shower

Another Bowdoin student said, "When I'm having trouble concentrating, I take a shower. There is something about a refreshing shower and a change of clothes that allows me to buckle down." Her peers in attendance both nodded in agreement.

Don't Move

One Bowdoin student told me that she liked to study in public areas among a group of known-to-be studious students. That way she would feel embarrassed if she kept getting up to talk, or get a cup of coffee, or get a drink of water. She found that she buckled down in this setting. She also found that she needed to stay put. Whenever she had study sessions where she would get up and move to a lounge in the library, then move to her room, then move to an isolated classroom building, all of those moves added up to her fooling herself. She invariably found that she got more work done if she didn't move.

The Internet and Gadgetry . . . Again

When I uttered the words "procrastination kills" to a Hobart student, he replied, "Yeah, and so do computers." He followed this up with "Beware of the Internet." As we've seen, all of my interviews made it clear that technology is a double-edged sword. You absolutely need to use it for thorough research, but you can also get trapped in it like quicksand as the opportunities for procrastination are endless.

While he was no fan of Facebook or cell phones when it came to class or study, a Tufts student did stress that he took full advantage of all the alarms on his cell phone and use them as a reminder to get back to work.

Start before You Start

A recent Rensselaer Polytechnic Institute grad told me about a system he devised in his mathematics classes. "You have to start before you start," he said. Sensing my puzzlement, he explained, "The instant the professor assigned the work during the class, I started doing it." He went on to say,

> I realized that all of the calculations he was doing on the board at any given moment related directly to the assignments he was giving us. He would tend to give us the next assignments in the final ten minutes of the class and would then make several references to them. I found that if I dove right in and started doing the calculations, I was a good part of the way to the conclusion, and then I would get back to my room and be able to do the work from a running start. Others around me would simply note the assignment and close their books for the day.

They later found themselves starting all over again when they sat down to do the work later that night.

Small Talks with Myself

A recent Colby College graduate told me that the thing that got her off the dime was something she called "small talks with myself."

She told me that she had grown up in China and come with her parents to live in Boston's Chinatown as a school girl. Suffice it to say that before she got to Colby, this young woman had been exposed to a variety of different cultural environments. After attending some of Boston's lowest performing public schools, she received the opportunity to spend her high school years at prestigious Boston Latin School, America's very first school. (Boston Latin was founded in 1635, one year before Harvard's founding.)

Colby's more rural location in a Maine town represented yet another cultural change. Furthermore, the approach to studying that she developed in high school tended toward a fastidious attention to detail that does not always work in college (college sometimes demands that you be able to skim reading assignments rather than read every single word). As she said, "I often felt overwhelmed in the early going. I initially assumed that I would simply do everything. I soon found out that I needed to prioritize but didn't know how. I sometimes felt paralyzed and wound up procrastinating."

She found that to rise above it all, she would have these small talks with herself and would also write in her journal. As an example, during her sophomore year she applied for a summer internship position with a Boston law firm. As part of the application process, she was expected to write an essay, and she kept putting it off. At the time, she wrote in her journal, "Focus on what you want, get moving, sit down, and start writing." So she followed through on her own advice and set to the task of writing the essay in pursuit of the internship. She believes that the combination of self-directed pep talk and notes in her journal helped her get down to business. She told me that she still has her journal and occasionally refers to it, even today.

Too Much Time

At one point as I neared the end of my interviews for this book, I found myself sitting around a table with three Bowdoin College undergraduates. When it came to procrastination, one observed, "The less time I have on my hands, the less time I procrastinate." The others agreed, and it dawned on me that this observation was nearly universal with all the college students I talked to. It is counterintuitive, but most of the students I spoke with found that a great deal of time leads to procrastination which in turn makes a strong case for the idea of committing to something to cut down on your idle time.

Like My Dad Did

Parents reading this book may have their hearts warmed by what another Bowdoin student said. He told me that he had always admired his dad's work ethic. He noticed that whenever his father had to produce a report or write an article, he had a process that he would engage in, and he would then sit down and do the task until it was completed. So, this student copies his dad! Author James Baldwin once said, "Children are never very good at listening to their elders, but they never fail to imitate them." There is something in this quote for new college students and their parents as well.

Procrastination: There's an App for That!

One Bowdoin College student answered my question about procrastination with a thoroughly modern answer, "There's an app for that." At first I thought he was kidding, and then he turned serious. Since this young man is a high honors student in a rigorous college curriculum, I thought I would listen. Sure enough, the app "Procrastination Killer" only costs $0.99, and it will disable sites like Facebook or your instant messaging capabilities for a specified length of time. Other similar anti-procrastination tools feature names like "Freedom" and "Self Control." While I'm a bit out of my element here, my understanding is that you determine the length of time you plan to study, set the app for that length of time, and you will be unable to use Facebook for that span during your study time—i.e., Facebook will be temporarily disabled. Others at the table agreed that an app like this is a valuable asset. Walking away I couldn't help but be overcome by a sense of irony. Here I had been trying to determine whether technology was a good or a bad thing when it comes to focused study, and these students clearly showed me that it's both.

VARIOUS PROCRASTINATION "THINGS"

During my discussions and interviews, some patterns (let's call them "things") began to emerge. Here are seven of them.

The Group Thing

A Notre Dame student was a big believer in group work as a way to fight procrastination. He noted that many of the business courses at Notre Dame involve group projects and acknowledged that sometimes participants in group projects don't end up with equal work loads. But he said, "For me, if I'm in a group I feel compelled to step up because I don't want to let anyone down. When I'm by myself, I can convince myself that I can slack off, but I can't convince the others in my study group that I can slack off." Once again, the Notre Dame student has developed a system that fits with what he has come to know about himself.

The Study Thing

A William & Mary grad observed, "When I figured out the study thing, I stopped procrastinating." When I pressed for an explanation, he cited a sense of satisfaction derived from getting things done ahead of time. For some reason, I began to beat paper and other assignment deadlines by two to three weeks. Some of this might have had something to do with the fact that I had gotten sick of my roommates! I'd never done that before. Not only did I feel good about my work ethic, my professors absolutely loved it, and I'm convinced that they also began to regard me as a very serious student. There was nothing but upside to that.

In a similar vein, a UNC Greensboro student spoke of what he called "the value of rough drafts." As he put it, "Procrastinating on editing is a lot better than procrastinating on doing." In other words (I think!), if you're going to procrastinate, know that some types of procrastination are of higher quality than others, and don't fall into the trap of trafficking in the cheaper grades.

The Visual Thing—Lists

A Colby grad observed, "I never really had those moments where I was desperately saying, 'Oh, Dear.' Maybe it's because I'm a compulsive list-maker. For me, there's just something about that visual thing where I'm able to say, 'OK, Let's check that one off the list right now.' Each check makes me feel a little bit better, like I'm staying ahead of the game."

He went on, "For some reason I was always just able to plod along. In fact, I remember a particularly challenging course— Comparative Politics—where I never worked so hard for a D. (And had never before received less than a B in anything.) I learned that if you just stay with it, you get where you need to go." I have to say, as an approach to procrastination, it's tough to beat that one.

A UNC Greensboro student said, "I hate the feeling of knowing that I'm not doing what needs to be done. One thing I do is keep all my course syllabi in a stack on my desk and check off the assignments as I do them. That way, I always have a window on what I need to do next, and those checks offer some level of satisfaction of completion as well as encouragement to move ahead."

The Financial Thing

Offering a piece of advice that might best fit the "Commit to Something" chapter, a George Mason University student advised, "Keep yourself busy, and you won't procrastinate. Also, the fact that I have a financial role in the whole experience helps strengthen my resolve. When you boil it all down, classes cost too much to skip."

The Team (and Friend) Thing

A Washington & Lee grad told me that the structure provided by his membership on the wrestling team helped out a lot in the procrastination department. He said, "I'm not sure how, but it helped me distinguish between 'work friends' and 'fun friends' and I was then able to align myself accordingly. Don't get me wrong, both types of friends are an important part of college. It's just that I found I needed to be sure that I was seeing the right ones at the right time." He also observed that he went into a bit of a downward spiral when an injury rendered him unable to compete one season: "I lost the structure, and my performance declined."

A Kenyon College basketball player experienced similar benefits: "I did a lot better in-season than out-of-season. She also expressed a repeating theme with students I spoke with: "When I only had forty-five minutes before practice I would tend to use that time to its fullest. However, on those occasions when I had the whole day free, for some reason, I might not manage to fit that little forty-five minutes into *any* point in the day."

The Third Party Thing

A Tufts student spoke of the value of a third party. He said, "When I have a paper due, I try to tell five or six people that I respect. As the date nears, they are likely to hassle me a bit by asking me how I'm doing on it—*So tell me, have you finished the first draft yet?*—and I don't want to have to say that I'm way behind. My little system helps give me a nudge when I'm likely to need it most. It forces me to move faster."

A George Mason student served up one from the Brutal Truths category when she said, "While college offers the chance to make a lot of friends of all shapes and sizes, make sure you have some relationships that are not superficial." By that, she means that you need to be sure to have some friends who will tell you the truth when you are slacking off too much. "You might not like it if and when they pull you aside and scold you to get to work, but chances are you'll thank them later."

The Pot Thing

When I closed out my discussion with him, a UNC Greensboro student said to me, "There's one more piece of advice I'd give to an incoming college student: Don't smoke pot every day." Chuckling, I assumed he was kidding with me. Turning serious, he went on to explain, "If you do smoke pot every day, there's a good chance that you'll flunk out of school. Not only that, but you won't remember much of what happened. So, if you're going to flunk out, you at least want to have some stories to tell. So, don't smoke pot every day and you will." Hmmm.

When I began this book, it never occurred to me how much fun the interviews would be. I also didn't expect to learn so much. I definitely would not have thought that I would come to see procrastination and flunking out in a whole new light. It would never have occurred to me that both phenomena have different levels of quality attached to them! But today, I'm here to tell you, they *do*.

OLD SCHOOL

In the course of writing this book, I focused my interviews on current college students and recent graduates in order to offer the freshest ideas possible. However, the truth of the matter is that some ideas are timeless. After all, there's probably a very good reason why they have stood the test of time. With this thought in mind, I started keeping track of my discussions with colleagues long since graduated. Many of them served up some approaches and techniques that are timeless. Here are a few.

The Research Paper: Step-by-Step

A teaching colleague of mine for twenty years recalls the approach he took to writing a paper during his undergraduate days at Massachusetts College of Liberal Arts:

The first week of class, when professors were handing out their syllabi, I immediately went to the test and research sections of the syllabi and marked a series of deadlines down on my calendar.

First Deadline: Before two weeks went by I would go to the professor's office to discuss the expectations he or she had for the paper and learn suggestions for books I might use in the research. After this discussion, I would go directly to the library and take out the books I would need for the research paper.

Second Deadline: I would pay another visit to the professor, bringing along the library books. This would often spark a useful discussion about the topic and would also demonstrate to the professor that I was serious about the paper and committed to doing my best.

Third Deadline: Over the next two weeks I would begin research-ing the paper, continually renewing the books. (You do not want to incur late fees!) I typically held the books until the paper was sub-mitted. This saved me from the frantic rush that typically goes on late in the semester when everyone is scrambling all at once to cram a semester's worth of research into a couple of weeks.

Fourth Deadline: At least three weeks before the paper was ac-tually due I was in typing mode. The computer lab was open and anything but crowded so I could take my time.

Fifth Deadline: One week before the final deadline I would visit the professor with my rough draft in hand. More often than not the professor was happy to view the paper and make final suggestions. I would then pass the paper in a few days later, a few days before the actual deadline.

In the end, I know that this process enabled me to submit my best work. I'm pretty sure that regardless of my writing style or the quality of my research, I tended to get a slightly better grade simply because of the fact that my professors felt I cared about my work.

Living Backwards

Another colleague, an excellent humanities teacher, gradu-ated from Bates College in the early 90s. He talks about a study technique that he calls "Living Backwards."

First, he stresses, "Know your reading speed." He reasoned that once he became a solid student, he could thoroughly read about 300 pages in a day. Knowing this, he would actually add up all of the pages in his reading assignments for the se-mester and determine how many study days he was going to need to get his work done. He would begin each day with the question "What's my day going to look like?" and knowing his reading speed helped him add a great deal of specificity in answering this question.

No Break Rule

My Bates colleague is also a proponent of what he calls the "No Break Rule." Simply put, he would sit down to study and say to himself, "I will not ____ until ____." The first blank could stand for anything from going to the bathroom, to getting a drink of water, to going for a cup of coffee. The second blank might be 100 pages of reading, 3 pages of writing, completion of a paper outline, etc.

A lot of people when they go to college bask in the absence of rules. Many come to find that rules are what keep them in line. Hey, it's one thing to have rules imposed upon you; it's another thing to design them and impose them on yourself. If you can't do that, you are probably going to have problems with a lot more than college. Speaking of rules . . .

AND THAT BRINGS US BACK TO RULE #1

To be sure, procrastination is not a habit that afflicts only college students. It can be a problem to anyone of any age. It lurks whenever humans need to do things like

- mow the lawn;
- pay the bills;
- make that dentist appointment;
- wash the car;

- write that thank-you note to that aunt who gave us that gift that we don't particularly like; and
- submit that final manuscript for the book you're writing about the first year of college.

Sometimes the outcomes of our procrastination are limited to mere embarrassment, like when we drive around town in a dirty car sporting graffiti that kids have traced into the dust on the hood with their fingers—e.g., *Wash Me!* Hey, maybe we just don't care if the neighbors gossip about how our lawn is the community eyesore.

On the other hand, those outcomes resulting from unpaid bills can bring bigger problems like repossessed cars and apartment evictions. Similarly, today's delayed dental check-up can sometimes evolve into tomorrow's root canal.

For you, a new college student, procrastination can lead to failing grades which are a problem no matter how you look at it:

- You'll hurt your GPA;
- You'll have to take the class all over again;
- You'll have to deal with angry parents who are upset over the prospect of having to pay for the same class again, especially when they are convinced that it had been within your power to pass it;
- You could even flunk out of school.

Anyway you slice it, all the outcomes from this scenario are bad.

The key is to get on top of your game and stay there. And consider the idea that the best way to do that might well be to simply return to the beginning of this book and . . . Go to Class!

I may not be able to prove it, but I'll bet heavily on the notion that there is a direct link between class attendance and procrastination. In other words, those who have big problems with procrastination will tend to have problems with class attendance AND those who make all their classes will tend to have their procrastination under control.

Not convinced? OK, how about a little experiment: Attend all your classes for the first semester and see how it impacts your procrastination. Let me know how it turns out.

"It was a party school."

Final Words from Elvis

So, when all is said and done, it's pretty simple:

1. CLASS—Go!
2. STUDY—3 x 5 = 15
3. COMMIT to something.
4. MENTOR—Get one.
5. PROCRASTINATION kills.

However, at some point we have to switch from talking about it to doing it. Although he never attended college, Elvis Presley seemed to understand when he sang:

"Don't procrastinate, Don't articulate . . .

A little less conversation, A little more action please."

I hope these five rules help you get the most out of what some say will be the best four years of your life. Good luck! But remember what 1st century Roman philosopher Seneca said, "Luck is what happens when preparation meets opportunity."

Onward,

Malcolm Gauld
Bowdoin College '76

Acknowledgments

First, I give special thanks to Ann Peden who helped me with typing, editing, and proofreading as she has done for many years now as my very own Professor of English Grammar.

I am also grateful for the editorial guidance provided by Tom Koerner of Rowman & Littlefield.

Thanks also to my colleagues at the Hyde Schools for their willingness to offer suggestions and criticism throughout this project. Risking the sin of omission, I single out Heather Cavalli, Bev Coleman, Joe Gauld (my dad), and Rose Mulligan.

Finally, special thanks to Laura Gauld, my wife, for her willingness to serve as a sounding board and contribute ideas. I pledge to do the same when you write your next book.

Collegiate Assistance

I could not have written this book without the anecdotes, ideas, and stories that were shared with me by scores of college students and graduates, many of them former students or current colleagues at the Hyde Schools. Experiences from the following colleges found their way into this book.

Bates College
Boston College
Bowdoin College
Colby College
Colgate University
College of William & Mary
Dickinson College
Franklin & Marshall College
Furman University
George Mason University
George Washington University
Gettysburg College

Hampshire College
Hartwick College
Haverford College
Hobart College
Kenyon College
Lawrence University
Lynchburg College
Massachusetts College of Liberal Arts
New York University
St. Lawrence University
Southern Methodist University
Springfield College
Tufts University
University of California, Berkeley
University of Denver
University of Maine
University of Maryland
University of New Hampshire
University of North Carolina, Greensboro
University of Notre Dame
University of Southern Maine
Vassar College
Washington College
Washington & Lee University
Wittenberg University
Worcester State College
Yale University

About the Author

Malcolm Gauld is president of the Hyde Schools, a national community of schools—private and public—committed to Hyde's unique brand of family-based character education. A graduate of Bowdoin College, he received his Master's Degree in Education from Harvard University. Malcolm and his wife Laura are the coauthors of *The Biggest Job We'll Ever Have*, a book intended to help parents raise children of strong character and families of purpose. They and their three children live in Bath, Maine.